PRAISE FOR *SEMPER VIRGO*

As we know, the dogma of the Perpetual Virginity of our Blessed Lady is one of the Four Marian dogmas of the Church, alongside the Immaculate Conception, the Assumption and the Motherhood of our Lady. We are grateful to Father Serafino Lanzetta for his reflections on the dogma of the Perpetual Virginity, and particularly how the dogma impacts the living out of chastity in the Sacrament of Marriage, celibacy in the priesthood, and chastity as lived in Consecrated Life. This timely book reveals a prayerful spiritual synthesis of Father Serafino's insights and implications for these states of life flowing from the dogma of Perpetual virginity.

— ✠**STEPHEN ROBSON**, (retired) Bishop of Dunkeld

The work of Fr. Lanzetta on Mary's virginity as the 'form' of Christianity shows the close relation of this Marian truth to the Incarnation of Christ and to Christian life. The dogma of the perpetual virginity of Mary is presented in its Biblical testimonies, defended against rationalist critiques, and rediscovered with the help of the Church Fathers.

— **FR. MANFRED HAUKE**, president of the German Society for Mariology, author of *Introduction to Mariology* (Washington, D.C.: CUA Press, 2021).

Father Serafino's recent study is, indeed, a study, something to be read, perhaps a few times. It is rich and deep. Like his study *Vatican II, A Pastoral Council*, it asks very precise questions about the language used in the conciliar documents and the subsequent problems that follow from the lack of the use of more precise terms. Ultimately, this careful investigation verifies a beautiful statement that the Fathers of the Second Vatican Council made: "Mary unites in her person and re-echoes the most important doctrines of the faith" (LG #65).

— **MSGR. ARTHUR B. CALKINS**, member of the Mariological Society of America, author of *Totus Tuus: Pope Saint John Paul II's Program of Marian Consecration and Entrustment* (New Bedford, MA: Academy of the Immaculate, 2017)

SEMPER VIRGO

Semper Virgo

MARY'S VIRGINITY AS THE "FORM" OF CHRISTIAN LIFE

Serafino M. Lanzetta

AROUCA
PRESS

ISBN: 978-1-990685-60-6 (pbk)
ISBN: 978-1-990685-61-3 (hc)

Arouca Press
PO Box 55003
Bridgeport PO
Waterloo, ON N2J 3G0
Canada
www.aroucapress.com

Send inquiries to info@aroucapress.com

*To Father Stefano M. Manelli and
Father Gabriele M. Pellettieri,
Founders of the Franciscans of
the Immaculate, Teachers
of Theology and Life*

CONTENTS

*T*HE TRUTH OF THE FAITH of the *perpetual virginity of Our Most Blessed Mother Mary* is in grave danger. This is the cry of alarm that emerges from this book, written to counter this danger and help us understand and shine a light on the purity and divine uniformity of the faith in the perpetual virginity of Our Most Blessed Mother Mary.

We cannot but extend at once our profound gratitude to the author of this theological study, Father Serafino Lanzetta, a prominent theologian in the forum of theology that is most committed to the defense of the Catholic Faith. He is, in fact, the editor of the prestigious journal of apologetics titled precisely *Fides Catholica*.

Those who wish to discover and begin to understand this most veritable doctrine of Catholic apologetics — the perpetual virginity of Our Most Blessed Mother Mary, a most exquisite and sublime truth of the Faith and a theological theme of prime importance and value — would do well to read this book with great attention. It is in fact a most suitable meditation for appreciating the radiant light of our unchangeable faith in the truth of the perpetual virginity of Our Most Blessed Lady.

Those who read and reflect on this book will find far more than they might expect. In its pages, there is an abundance of dogmatic, biblical, patristic, moral, spiritual, and Marian theology — and still more. In sentence after sentence, with precise terminology and a firm style, Father Lanzetta's thought never deviates from the substance of the main theme, regardless of the varying intensity with which it is examined.

With few but forceful chapters, set against today's bleak "Marian minimalism," this study by Lanzetta is very much needed, as it retraces the Church's faith in the perpetual virginity of Our Most Blessed Lady through the various stages of its history; in so doing, it restores this truth to its pure and constant blueprint as the "form of Christ and Christians" (p. 42), "configured as the most perfect way of living the Christian vocation in this world given its conformity to the lives of Jesus and the Ever-Virgin Mary" (p. 15).

The life of a consecrated virgin, being conformed to the lives of Jesus and Mary, carries within itself the primacy of complete supremacy and excellence over that of married life, something that was already solemnly defined as a dogma by the Council of Trent.[1]

In the four chapters of this book, the author presents the entire patrimony of Mary's perpetual virginity as a truth of the Faith, a truth enclosed in the mystery of the divine maternity with which the person of Mary Ever-Virgin is endowed, along with her entire life as virgin *before*, *during*, and *after* the birth of the Incarnate Word.

The themes and topics that emerge from this most exquisite divine mystery of Mary's perpetual virginity are numerous and wide ranging. Indeed, this mystery runs throughout Sacred Scripture, covering the entire intertestamental scheme of the Bible. It is transmitted and then explained by the entire patristic tradition of the first millennium, by Church tradition in the second millennium, and continuing this day until the end of time — always monitored in its enduring purity of faith and sound doctrine by the highest levels of the Church Magisterium.

It is essential, however, to be on guard assiduously against the errors that violate this heavenly mystery, since we can be sure that undermining this truth means undermining and compromising also the other truths of the Faith that are in divine harmony with it, starting with the sublime truth of the mystery of the Incarnation of the Word in the Immaculate Virgin.

Father Lanzetta sifts through old and new errors with watchful care, invariably and intelligently drawing them back to the most clear-cut and measured interpretation — an interpretation that is always faithful to its perennial and unchangeable biblical and dogmatic foundations and that, at times, delves deeply into the more sublime and extensive elements of grace for our benefit, as ever needy creatures.

Moreover, a special skill of Father Lanzetta's is his ability to shed light on a truth of the Faith by using statements of principle that facilitate the understanding and recollection of even very lofty teachings, which he then synthesizes into a few concise and clear sentences. For example, he writes that Mary's virginity:

• *"Is the golden thread stitching together all the elements of the Christian Faith"* (p. 1).
• *"Is the font of perfection for all states of Christian life"* (p. 9).
• Is the *"public sign of toto corde union with God"* (p. 34).
• Is the *"form of Christianity"* (p. 8, 48).
• Is the *"forma sanctitatis"* (p. 49).
• Is the superior *"form"* that unites virginity and martyrdom (p. 56).
• Is the superior *"form"* that unites virginity and spousal love (p. 51).
• Is the *"hermeneutical key of the 'Kingdom of God' in Christ"* (p. 110).

Aided by Father Lanzetta's book and the staunch, ardent faith in the divine Ever-Virgin Mother contained in its pages, which echo the Gospel Revelation's portrayal of the always miraculously intact Virgin *before*, *during*, and *after* the birth of the Incarnate Word, may we praise ever more the Most Holy Mother of God and our Mother: the *Ever-Virgin Mother!*

Fr. Stefano M. Manelli

INTRODUCTION

"Quando natus es ineffabiliter ex Virgine, tunc impletae sunt Scripturae; sicut pluvia in vellus descendisti, ut salvum faceres genus humanum: te laudamus, Deus noster."[1]

ARY'S VIRGINITY IS the golden thread that stitches together all the elements of the Christian Faith. It is intertwined with the Christological mystery, and for this reason, it is *one* with the central dogma of the Faith: the Incarnation of the Word. So much so, that if Mary's virginity is denied, the Incarnation itself is also disbelieved, and vice versa. To attack, downgrade, or revise the mystery of Mary's virginity means nothing less than attempting to redefine the mystery of the Incarnate Word in ways that are more acceptable to modern, itching ears (cf. 2 Tim. 4:3).

Unfortunately, it is not always the case that what people want to hear is also true. Hence, throughout the history of the Church, there has been no lack of reductionist threats regarding the mystery of Mary's virginity. In ancient times, as in recent times, a sort of *nouvelle vague* presenting Mary in a "new" or "renewed" way, at times better suited to man's worldly aspirations, has ended up discarding the sound doctrine perennially taught by the Church.

Such an "up-to-date" way of addressing Mary's mystery has often resulted in a ditching of the very same mystery and a loss of understanding of how important virginity and chastity are for the Kingdom of Heaven. Nowadays, it seems that those words of our Lord exhorting us to renounce all for the sake of the Gospel, even our own bodies, are merely words of another age, an age long since buried under the debris of an arrogant, rigid, manualistic theology. The Church is being asked, for example, to reconsider the mystery of ecclesiastical celibacy, playing on the fact that it is not a definitive dogma but merely a disciplinary item connected to the priesthood. This increasingly widespread appeal, which lately seems even inclined to exploit the numerous grave scandals of pedophilia and especially ephebophilia (despite them having no causal link to ecclesiastical celibacy), neglects an essential fact: celibacy arose not as a prohibition to marry but as the way to achieve perfect continence for the Kingdom of Heaven. Manipulating its identity by making it appear as the mere disciplinary intransigence of a medieval Church, aside from not solving the problem of shrinking vocations, manifests the void of meaning smiting today's Church. It is the very same hollowness that leads to the sexual abuse among the clergy — that is, the hollowed-out meaning of the value of chastity and purity, both echoes of Mary's virginity.

Another modern-day maneuver, alongside the revisionist attempt to reinterpret ecclesiastical celibacy, is that of reducing the indissolubility of marriage to a mere temporal consideration and to a responsible choice. Giving Holy Communion to the divorced and remarried presupposes this reduction, even if presented on a case-by-case basis under the mantle of pastoral kindness. Even prior to this recent revisionism, religious life had been demeaned to a mere life-choice option for Christians, one among many. The concept of Christian perfection has been watered down, with religious life no longer portrayed as the "state of perfection." And as a result, marriage is also suffering.

We shall try to call out these itchings for novelty, and the resulting theological twists and turns, by going straight to the heart of the problem and pointing out, by way of contrast, the perennial relevance of the fundamental truth of Holy Mary's virginity. Theological discernment and concordance within Holy Scripture already map out in the person of Mary Ever-Virgin, as in a template, the evangelical elements concerning the proclamation of God's Kingdom and its fulfillment in Christ.

We believe that the issue at the heart of the current crisis in the Church is rooted in a superficial, reductionist Christian vision, alongside a biased exegetical and theological reading of the mystery of her who is the Mother of all Christians and their model within the Church. She is the model because she is the form, or mold, of Christians. There are certainly also other reasons, but these seem to be at the root. Mary's virginity is the pure womb of the Church, the immaculate womb in which all vocations are formed interdependently, vivified by the Spirit, and propelled to gaze at the "things above" (see Col. 3:1) by her who has always been there above.

In this work, prompted by some new exegetical propositions, we aim to examine whether the thesis that tarnishes the mystery of Mary's virginity is sustainable in the light of all of Scripture, as it developed from the oral tradition, or whether, for theological-exegetical reasons that we will readily highlight as hermeneutical keys for a correct understanding of the Kingdom of God, such a thesis appears instead to belittle the entire Christian mystery. The misunderstanding of Mary's virginity in Raymond E. Brown's works prompts us to attempt to read the mystery of Mary's virginity as the *key* to understanding the entire Christian message and, above all, as a bastion in defense of the truth of God's Kingdom residing in the person of Christ—as the possibility for God's Kingdom to establish itself among men and as the promise of entry into it for all those of good-will. This Kingdom, which is the presence of God reigning in our midst (see Luke 17:21), begins with the mystery of Mary's virginity, with Jesus's virginal conception from Mary. Herein is the *form*, the formation of Christ's being as true man and of everyone that is reborn in Christ as a child of the Father in Heaven.

The mystery of Mary's virginity is the assurance of the primacy of God in the world. It is proof that the Kingdom brought about by Christ begins in the spirit and not in the flesh—"God is a spirit" (John 4:24)—so as to ennoble the flesh and elevate the whole man into a higher dimension, that of the Kingdom in its fullness, where God will be "all in all" (1 Cor. 12:6). Mary is the virginal womb safeguarding the mystery of Christ and the Church, enshrining it as in a treasure chest.

Most importantly, St. Ambrose dedicated marvelous pages to the virginal bond between Christ and Mary, which foreshadows the mystery of the Church. If, as he says, the body of a virgin consecrated to God is the *temple* of God,[2] how much more impressive and sacred was the body of Mary, true temple of the Most High, in which the Son of God dwelt physically?[3] For the saintly bishop of Milan, Mary is the model of virgins since she is "the icon of virginity,"[4] an icon that then reflects itself onto the spousal Church. The virgin is so noble as to be a *typus* or even a *sacramentum Ecclesiae*,[5] whose deepest cause is yet to be found in her being Mother of Our Lord,[6] "figure" and "presence" of the Church in the order of faith, of charity, and of perfect union with Christ.

St. Jerome adds a pearl of wisdom that also considers the priestly dimension of Christ. Referring to Mary's perpetual virginity, he equates it with the "east gate" of Jerusalem's Temple, which always remained closed because the Lord had passed through it (see Ez. 44:1–2). This is the gate that would veil or unveil the Holy of Holies. Through it, "the Sun of justice" (Mal. 4:2), Christ, our High Priest according to the order of Melchizedek (see Heb. 5:10), is the One who enters and exits, though the gate remains sealed and always resplendent.[7]

With good reason, then, St. Athanasius could say candidly that virginity entered the world through Mary,[8] just as Christ entered the world through the Virgin Mary. St. Augustine, echoing him, writes, "Virginal dignity had its beginnings with the Mother of God."[9]

To these Church Fathers, we need to add a great Byzantine Father, St. Maximus the Confessor, in his *Life of Mary*, writes, "Truly She alone is a virgin exalted above all other virgins, an ever-immaculate virgin: before the birth, during the birth, and after the birth. Further, she was not only given the grace of perpetual virginity, but from that instant onwards she became the foundation of virginity for other women, and, through her, the capacity was given to women who desire to be virgins."[10]

We can read the Gospel in the resplendent light of the Ever-Virgin Mary and thereby realize the relevance of Christ's message. Her virginity is the ever ancient and ever new timeless today of the One Incarnate Word ready to take root in our life. Only if we safeguard intact the mystery of Mary's perpetual virginity will our eyes be sufficiently clear-sighted to contemplate God and hope in salvation. If, on the contrary, we show contempt for it — or worse, water it down, rendering it a "theologoumenon" (a mere narrative construct of the theological idea of Christ's divine sonship), where theology is no longer incarnated in history and thus has nothing more to say to today's world — soon the truth of the entire Christian mystery, in all its breadth and depth, will be obscured.[11]

In this latter case, we will remain in the Church, but she will have been transformed into a pious association of good men, performing many good works but unable to see beyond the wretched humanity that dwells within us and the rest of men. Even the Eucharist will become mere "bread for the poor" (from the

Panis Angelicus), the vision of a theologically weak mindset that dilutes the real presence of the Lord, equating it to a mere memory of God's love; while marriage, even if still valued as an ideal to be pursued, will have nothing more to say to us other than that man and woman are not indissolubly made for one another but rather at the service of each other, according to the fashions of the time, which means marriage becomes a purely human affair. What is missing is a transcendent perspective, a vision that goes beyond the confines of that ephemeral realm now apparently being discussed by academics and having priority in pastoral agendas. What is missing is a surge of freshness, of purity.

At times, one gets the impression that we have become so accustomed to the ways of the world that we have nearly grown used to the corruption of sin and can now no longer shake it off. While the anthropological revolution has been accomplished in the Church, man has lost an essential aspect of his being: his soul. Left unattended, it is now practically dead. By undoing the chastity of love, we have lost the sense of truth; by abandoning the truth that virginity is superior to all the other states in life, we have leveled out everything to the point of eliminating all distinctions. Now there are no longer any differences left because there is nothing more to distinguish. Even the *signs* of God have been obscured, and we are no longer able to understand them.

We find a clear affirmation of our Christian belief, contrary to what those in the past or present are eager to repudiate, in the words of St. Ildefonsus of Toledo when defending our Lady's virginity against the Jews. These are very timely words, which go beyond the Jewish context of his time and compel everyone to reflect on one fundamental matter: What unique sign, announced by the prophets and proclaimed by Old Testament figures, would the Lord have offered if a young married woman and not a virgin had given birth? What would the miracle and its uniqueness consist in?[12] Obviously, one cannot simply reject the miracle out of principle or bias, and we must instead move from a socio-political consideration of the "sign" to one rooted in wisdom literature and theology.

Mary's virginal consecration to God rises like the dawn of the new covenant, the principle of salvation, the prospect of God becoming Emmanuel, God-with-us. For Him to be with us, but most of all for us to be with Him, it is essential that we safeguard the untainted virginity of His Mother.

This is precisely what we wish to proclaim from these pages: that the Virgin Mary is our assurance for remaining faithful to the truth of Christ's Gospel. Her virginity is *the form* of Christianity, the untainted essence of Christian life, that which informs sanctifying grace and will confer a proper existence to all states of life, uniting them harmoniously within a deep-seated hierarchy, at whose highest level is that which is the most perfect: the virginity of Christ and of Mary. These are followed by the religious vocation and that of the celibate priesthood and celibate lay life, then by widowhood chosen for the love of Christ, and lastly, by Matrimony, with its call to live in conjugal chastity in imitation of Mary's spiritual virginity by remaining faithful to the primary end of marriage, pro-creation, creating for God and with God. This hierarchy of perfection hinges on Mary's virginity. Vice versa, Mary's virginity is the font of perfection for all states of Christian life, all of which are connected to Mary's virginal birth.

With this, we would like to echo an ancient and much-loved reflection of the great saint of Hippo, who writes thus:

> Rejoice, virgins of Christ, for the mother of Christ is your sister. You could not have been mothers of Christ in the flesh, but for the love of Christ you have not desired to be mothers of any child. He who was not born of you was born for you. However, if you remember his words, as you should, you know that you are His mother because you do the will of His Father. For He Himself has said: "Whoever does the will of my Father is my brother and sister and mother."
>
> Rejoice, widows of Christ, for you have vowed holy continence to Him who made virginity fruitful. Rejoice, you who are chaste in marriage, living faithfully with your husbands; treasure in your hearts what you have lost in the body. Since your body cannot be free from conjugal contact, may your conscience remain intact in faith even as the whole Church is virginal.
>
> In Mary, consecrated virginity brought forth Christ; in Anna, aged widowhood recognized the Christ-child; in Elizabeth, conjugal chastity and fertility in old age were put to good use for Christ.
>
> All classes of faithful members have brought to their head what by his grace they were able to give. In like manner do you, because Christ is truth and

peace and justice, conceive him in faith and show him forth in works. Let your heart accomplish in the law of Christ what Mary's womb wrought in the flesh of Christ. How are you not included in the childbearing of Mary since you are the members of Christ? Mary brought forth your head; the Church, you, his members. For the Church, too, is both mother and virgin: mother by the bowels of charity, virgin by the integrity of faith and piety. She brings forth diverse peoples, but they are members of him whose body and spouse she is, and even in this respect she bears the likeness of the Virgin because in the midst of many she is the mother of unity.[13]

Mary's virginity, as *form*, confers perfection to the Christian being. She is not only the quintessential "type" but also what the Divine Agent has in mind as the end of all creation when imbuing goodness and original purity in the good things created by Him — a creation willed and forever safeguarded as immaculate in Mary despite the sin of man. Mary is the *form*, as St. Maximus the Confessor says, because not only through her "was virginity planted in humanity" but also it is always through her that "we are endowed by God and have been united to Him, and He has given us power to become children of God."[14]

In her, we are preserved from itching for novelty and the craving for worldly success that water down the Faith, the sacraments, and the mystery of the Church, virgin and mother. Mary marks the *beginning*, and every new beginning cannot but start from her and echo anew her immaculate *fiat* to God, the dawn of salvation.

CHAPTER I

Christian Perfection for Everyone and the Choice of "My God and My All"

"Christus virgo, virgo Maria, utrique sexui
virginitatis dedicavere principia."[15]

THE STATES OF LIFE
"If thou wilt be perfect..." (Matt. 19:21)

W
E WILL BEGIN BY addressing at length the important question of how the various states of Christian life relate to virginity or perfect chastity consecrated to God, the supreme good praised by the Church from time immemorial. A notable change in Church teaching on this question has in our view caused a realignment that has led to an increase in instability and loss of identity while the promised fruits of the Church's teaching have yet to arrive.

Traditionally, among the different states of life — religious, priestly, and lay — the religious state used to be considered the state of evangelical perfection. This is because the religious are most inclined to Gospel perfection through their religious vows and actions — namely, their profession of the evangelical counsels of poverty, chastity, and obedience. This does not, however, imply that religious people are necessarily "superior" to lay people, or that they will necessarily achieve higher levels of sanctity. Moreover, the religious state of life, configured as the most perfect way of living the Christian vocation in this world, given its conformity to the lives of Jesus and the Ever-Virgin Mary, also shows that Gospel perfection is already achievable in this life, and not just in the next. After all, when addressing that young man who wanted to follow Him, in addition to keeping the commandments, Jesus said to him, "If thou wilt be perfect, go sell what thou hast, and give to the poor, and thou shalt have treasure in heaven: and come follow me" (Matt. 19:21).

The adjective "perfect" is rendered from the Greek with *téleios* (from *telos*), in the sense of possessing all that is needed to achieve completeness. Admittedly, the same invitation to perfection is seen also in Matthew 5:48, where Jesus, referring to everyone, says, "Be ye therefore perfect, as also your heavenly Father is perfect." Being perfect like the Father is rendered with the same adjective that indicates completeness. St. Paul afterwards will say the same — for example, in Romans 12:2 — when exhorting all Christians not to conform to the mentality of this world but instead allow themselves to be transformed so that they can discover what is pleasing and perfect according to God's will. It is in fact a call to "arrive at the unity of faith, and of the knowledge of the Son of God, unto a perfect man, unto the measure of the fullness of Christ" (Eph. 4:13; here also, "perfect" is rendered with the same Greek word). At the same time, a significant difference can be easily noticed. The rich young man *is invited* to be perfect *now* by doing what Jesus has advised him to do — namely, leaving everything for the sake of His love and following Him, and thereby finding the perfect *sequela Christi*. By contrast, in the other cases, Jesus invokes the importance of striving for Christian perfection, and this call to strive for holiness is portrayed as imperative, as a precept to follow, as something to be achieved.

The goal of Christian life is the perfection of charity by adherence to charity's precept: to love God with all one's heart and one's neighbor as oneself (see Deut. 6:4–5; Matt. 22:37). The commandments are the necessary means (*ad esse*) to reach this goal. Religious vows — "if you want to be perfect" — are useful but not strictly necessary in this regard, but rather something extra (*ad bene esse*), that "special plus" in the Christian life in terms of visible conformity to Christ. Here the verb used by our Lord is in the present indicative tense.[16]

Being as perfect as our heavenly Father will surely require a journey of fidelity to Christ, an entire life of conformity to Him through performing interior acts of virtue; and in any case, the acquired perfection will be only a distant participation of that of the Father. The perfection of a religious does not consist in the acquired holiness, as in this regard both religious and the laity alike are called to holiness. Rather, it is the religious rule under which he lives that places him in a privileged and superior position to acquire holiness compared to any other state of life because of the public acts he performs. These public acts tend to perfect virtue; however, unlike for the lay person, the acts of a religious are, in addition those that are interior, primarily exterior and visible, and hence always recognizable as such.

Just as the sacrifice of the Lord is an interior act of obedience to the Father, which corresponds to the immolation of His body, so it is also for the religious, who is not holier than a lay person just because he is a religious but because he is placed in a more perfect state of life, a state more conformed to Christ's oblation. This still does not mean that a religious person will be necessarily more perfect than a lay person in the Kingdom of Heaven, as it is the individual holiness achieved by each of them on earth that will determine their level of contemplation of God in paradise. It simply means that the religious life is, in and of itself, a more perfect state of life than lay life.[17]

The ultimate reason for this superiority and excellence consists in the fact that virginity is superior to Matrimony. If, therefore, the religious fails to become holy, he will be doubly responsible before the heavenly Father and will almost always fall extremely low, dragging many others down with him. Having lost the concept of "sacrifice" in Christian life, we have also lost the notion of religious life as a "holocaust" for God. Hence its impoverishment.

THE "COUNSEL" OF THE APOSTLE PAUL

St. Paul's discourse on virginity's excellence and his assurance that "it is a good thing not to touch a woman," must be framed within his broader teaching on the body being the temple of the Holy Spirit (see 1 Cor. 6:19–20). The Christian man has been redeemed from God at the great price of Christ's most precious Blood. As the body is sanctified by the Holy Spirit, impurity is directly contrary to the body's dignity, even though every sin he commits is outside the body. St. Paul's admonition to "glorify and bear God in your body" (1 Cor. 6:20) is directed at everyone, men and women, married or celibate. For him, the body shares in a personal dignity since it does not serve a merely external function, a function it would have been confined to if it was just like a dispensable shell surrounding the soul, as was believed in pagan cultures. Indeed, the body is elevated to the point where we can aim very much higher and where it can be cherished even in perfect chastity.

This is how chapter 7 of the First Letter to the Corinthians is introduced, whereby the Apostle, who had taken a vow of celibacy himself, begins by saying that "it is a good thing for a man not to touch a woman" (1 Cor. 7:1). Almost as if wanting to draw a parallel between this counsel and the Creator's verdict who "saw that [each thing that he had created] was a good thing" (Gen. 1:4).[18] It seems as though we are hearing an echo here, that his advice concerning virginity is a good thing that is pleasing to the Creator. The Apostle gives advice along these lines since he knows it is not at odds with God's will, and what is more, it is no doubt advice that he himself has put into practice. Hence his stunning testimonial: "For I would that all men were even as myself" (1 Cor. 7:7) — that is, celibate ("even as I am" 1 Cor. 7:8)[19] for the Lord, to be one with Christ and thus able to say, "And I live, now not I; but Christ liveth in me" (Gal. 2:20).

Nonetheless, here the Apostle to the Gentiles makes a particularly important clarification: "May each receive from God their gift [*kárisma*], one in one way, one in another" (1 Cor. 7:7). The states of life are not opposed to one another, but each is a *charism* that comes from the Creator at the service of the others. There is no conflict among the diverse ways of living the Christian vocation, and the call to perfect holiness stands as a requirement for everyone. Even so, the Apostle's yearning could still strike a chord because to be like him would have spared the married those tribulations of the flesh (see 1 Cor. 7:28). Once more, this is a reference to his status as a eunuch for the Kingdom of Heaven: "To the unmarried, and to the widows: It is good for them if they so continue, even as I." (1 Cor. 7:8); in other words, if they too keep an undivided heart for the Lord.

And finally, because the condition St. Paul experiences in his own flesh is "a good thing," we have his "counsel:" "Now concerning virgins, I have no commandment of the Lord; but I give counsel, as having obtained mercy of the Lord, to be faithful" (1 Cor. 7:25); in other words, just like one who has received the grace of being a eunuch for the Gospel (cf. Matt. 19:12).

Despite highlighting that marrying is a *charism* and not something sinful (see 1 Cor. 7:28) since Matrimony is a sacred mystery, even the married ought to strive towards the final manifestation of eternal glory by living as if they were not married. For the fashion of this world passes away. Although marriage is a good in and of itself, it is, however, directed toward a greater good: the attainment of eternal life. St. Paul tells the Corinthians that, even when married, they should be watchful in seeking to please the Lord in all things, remaining oriented towards Him, to overcome the inevitable divisions of the heart.

In this regard, married people have a role model in the virgin who "thinketh on the things of the Lord, that she may be holy both in body and in spirit" (1 Cor. 7:34). That is why, returning once more to the excellence of virginity and chastity for God's Kingdom, St. Paul voices again his youthful longing to see the Corinthians free of anxieties so that they can concern themselves solely with the things of the Lord and with how to please Him (see 1 Cor. 7:32). St. Paul's words—"For I would that all men were even as myself" (1 Cor. 7:7)—are heard at this point in his advice to virgins who concern themselves entirely with the things of the Lord and how they can please Him alone. He wishes that everyone could choose continence to anticipate eternal life right now and to remain striving towards it unceasingly. With the certainty that everyone has received their own particular charism, what matters for both the celibates and the married is to bring it to fruition—with the same awareness that life is short, that the fashions of this world are destined to pass, and that only the eternity of Christ's love remains forever. Only Christ endures, the rest passes away. Relative things like Matrimony, the use of the goods of the world, joy, and grief too (see 1 Cor. 7:29–31) must be subject to absolute things, to union with the Lord in both body and soul.

The supremacy of virginity stems from the ongoing tension between the reality of existing as a discrete being and the need to be at one with the Lord. The complementarity and hierarchy of the various Christian states of life must be understood within this virtuous tension. Christianity gives Matrimony a place of honor with equal dignity to man and woman, a message that is truly disruptive to pagan culture and that echoes the *ipsissima verba Christi* (the very own words of Christ). It declares for the first time that the body of the husband is the property of the wife and vice versa, and that the wife must not be separated from her husband, but that if she does decide to separate, she must not marry again (see 1 Cor. 7, 4, 10–11). Moreover, both spouses are called to live marriage according to a superior dimension: that of Christ's love for us to the very end. This will transform the spousal union into a state of matrimonial chastity, with transmission of life as its primary end.

St. Paul's celibacy and the good example of virgins would become the preferential guidelines of the early Church, the church of Corinth and all the other churches that would come into existence through the preaching of the Apostles, who left everything (cf. Luke 5:11) for Christ. In essence, virginity and celibacy would become not just an ideal to pursue but a concrete model for the Christian life, its archetype, the means to safeguard all the other charisms and states of life with which the Lord enriches His Church. And of course, each and all of them are rejoined "vertically" in Christ, finding perfect unity solely above, in their union with Him.

Therefore, according to the Pauline theology that can be inferred from First Corinthians, virginity and celibacy appear foundational for the Church and for Christian life. Why is this? What lies behind this conviction? Why does the Apostle to the Gentiles bring to the fore repeatedly his own example, yearning for all to be like him and presenting himself as someone "worthy of trust" when counseling virgins?

One line of enquiry could undoubtedly be one of the initial and foundational truths of Christianity itself: Christ is "made of a woman" (Gal. 4:4) — that is, born virginally, solely from a woman, without the concourse of man.[20] This would have been a very strange idea for such an eloquent authority on Rabbinic culture as Paul of Tarsus and for Hebrew customs, according to which it is only men, and not women, who can generate. But Saul, now as Paul, must have learned of Christ's virginal conception. With the Virgin Mary, something unheard of and shocking is being fulfilled: a woman who generates the Son of God according to the flesh because she is a virgin, rendered so by the action of the Holy Spirit.

St. Matthew's genealogy is witness to this (see Matt. 1, 16). Christ is thereby made *ex muliere*, solely through Mary by the work of the divine Paraclete. This would later resound in the faith of the Church when the Nicene Creed professes that the Son of God became incarnate *"de Spiritu Sancto ex Maria Virgine."*

The icon of the Virgin Mother, of she who gives birth to the Son of God while remaining forever virgin, is so well imprinted in the Apostle Paul's mind and heart that the life of his Corinthian community would inevitably be modeled upon it. For St. Paul, the Ever-Virgin Mary is somehow the template and form of Christian life since it embodies the character of maternity, and consequently of the human spousal mystery and of virginity. Virginity envelops her maternity and would become also for St. Paul the means of exercising his apostolic paternity towards all peoples entrusted to his ministry, living as Christ did and choosing to be one with Him in celibacy.

Objectively, St. Paul's thinking on virginity, and his advice to virgins who choose Christ above all else, cannot but derive from the fact that Jesus was born solely of a woman — in other words, that Jesus is the fruit of His Mother's virginity. Here we have the original template and form. The virgins who follow this example embody the example of the Virgin Mother in time: they bring Jesus to the light of day by maintaining their integrity in His service, while becoming a model for the entire Church of how to follow Christ by embodying the most perfect love. Matrimony is not antithetical to virginity, nor is virginity against the good of marriage, but nonetheless what transpires clearly is that for the charisms bestowed by God, their hierarchy needs to be given priority over their complementarity. This hierarchy does not concern perfection as such but the means ordered towards achieving it.

We will understand this better by looking first at the Magisterium and then at the theological work that was undertaken to bring about the renewal deemed necessary to improve our understanding of the various states of life in relation to the universal call to holiness.

A SIGNIFICANT CHANGE

The doctrine of the excellence of the life of perfect chastity for the Kingdom of Heaven was reiterated in recent times by Pius XII in the apostolic constitution *Provida Mater Ecclesia*, with which he gave recognition also to the secular institutes. In it, he reaffirms that the Church, always faithful to Christ her spouse, had adapted to the times the doctrine of "the state of perfection" uninterruptedly until the then promulgated *Code of Canon Law* (1917). The Church's particular attention was "directed chiefly to public profession properly so called"[21]—namely, what the angelic shepherd defines as the "canonical state of perfection" to which the religious belong, a state recognized as "of one of the three chief ecclesiastical states of life,"[22] which the Church had made into its second order and grade.

And, "the existing 'orders of canonical persons' were considered to arise by divine law from the nature of the Church as hierarchically constituted and structured: to these was thus added an ecclesiastical institution (canons 107, 108/3). This class, 'religious,' a state between the two and compatible with either, was created for no other reason than that it is closely identified with the essential purpose of the Church, sanctification effectually sought in ways congruous to so sublime a purpose."[23]

Lumen gentium, by contrast, prefers to speak about the religious state as simply a "special gift in the life of the Church,"[24] which is no longer an intermediate order between clergy and the laity insofar as some faithful from either of them may be called to become part of it[25] and for the fact that, as stated in the new *Code of Canon Law*, the state of consecrated life is by its very nature neither clerical nor lay[26] but "belongs to the life and holiness of the Church."[27] In *Lumen gentium*, religious life is placed after the laity (chapter 4) and after the universal call to holiness (chapter 5).

Thus, the emphasis on the universal call to holiness, along with considering the religious life merely as "a special gift," but one lacking the theology of perfection of the religious state, has led many theologians to interpret the new magisterial position as a reduction of the value of consecrated life and of its excellence compared to the other states of life.

In the post-synodal apostolic exhortation *Vita consecrata*, John Paul II sought to bring back religious life to the well-established canonical rank it had held since the origins of Christianity, rooted in the example of Christ: virgin, poor, and obedient. In the words of Pope John Paul II, with the profession of these evangelical counsels, the religious ensures that these "characteristic features of Jesus" are "made permanently 'visible' in the midst of the world."[28] The same exhortation reaffirmed — albeit with just one reference — the concept of the "way or state of perfection" applied to the religious life, starting from the fact that "the Church has always seen in the profession of the evangelical counsels a privileged path to holiness."

The expressions that define such a profession, such as "the school of the Lord's service, the school of love and holiness, the way or state of perfection, indicate both the effectiveness and richness of the means which are proper to this form of evangelical life, and the special commitment made by those who embrace it."[29]

Sure enough, however, after the Second Vatican Council, consecrated life underwent an unprecedented crisis of indescribable proportions.[30] Then again, this crisis soon also toppled the recognition of the true identity of marriage. The frightening collapse of vocations, accompanied by a massive outflow of religious from the immediate post-council time until today, is the visual manifestation of this crisis. This crisis cannot be overcome by simply blaming a change in society, or by seeing the tragic closures of monasteries and convents as a voluntary "exodus," or as a moment of epoch-making, and mostly theological, transition towards the promised land of equality for all the baptized and of a yet to come renewal of consecrated life.

According to such thinking, the present impoverishment of the consecrated life has now even become the "theological locus" of God's will. His will would say to consecrated men and women that, while in the nineteenth-century religious orders were needed to address the social difficulties of that time, now, instead, there is the need to take care of the bedridden and the disabled.[31] These are rather the reflections that emerge at a point of destitution, including a dearth of sound theology. And this at a time when the mission of the Church has been crushed and flattened, and when the zeal for the salvation of souls, along with the servicing of various human needs, including social ones, has lost its energy and drive.

The new motto is "living is moving," because now we are all supposed to be travelers, and "the traveler is the one who leads us continuously to take 'another little step,' both as individuals and as a community, since we cannot consider ourselves in any way in a 'state of perfection,' since we believe that another world, another person, another religious life is possible, and that the Lord Jesus guides history."[32]

The ultimate consequence of living permanently in a process of continuous becoming, as if in an "exodus," is that the consecrated life can basically become anything at any time, even the opposite of itself.

In our view, the crux of the crisis of consecrated life lies precisely in the abandonment of the concept of the "state of perfection." It is now time to stop blaming others and especially a society that differs from the time when large families produced many vocations for the Church. The time has come to begin to reflect seriously on the theological roots of the crisis of religious life.

If Christian families are no longer large, undoubtedly this is also due to a theological and moral shift in doctrine that has repercussions in the shortage of religious vocations. But it is also true that the loss of the notion of religious life, as a life of perfection, has contributed to a slackening of the call to conjugal morality for matrimonial chastity — namely, to the openness to life as the primary end of marriage. The perfection of charity in the religious life is in crisis, as the sociological survey of religious life over these past fifty years clearly shows. Since this crisis is principally due to a breakdown in the perfect chastity required for God's Kingdom, marriage also cannot but suffer a breakdown as it strives to transcend the bonds of flesh and blood to open itself up to God's will.

THEOLOGIANS GRAPPLING WITH RENEWAL
After the council, various theologians have sought to find a solution to the states of life issue and to overcome some of the differences between the state of virginity or celibacy and the married state by seeking to harmonize the pursuit of Christian perfection. Unless restored into a virtuous unity, these two avenues risk delineating and setting side by side two categories of persons: those consecrated to God and married people, with marriage becoming a sort of safety net for those unable to live Christian perfection in the most perfect state of life.

In an agenda-setting article in 1977, the Carmelite priest Antonio Sicari pursues a lengthy investigation that presents a solution to the issue, starting with patristic theology and then passing on to newer theology.[33] In a thorough examination of the Church Fathers concerning the excellence of virginity and the role of marriage, Sicari reaches the following perfectly respectable conclusion: "The expression of Schillebeeckx that we cited, whereby it is not virginity, but marriage that needs justification,[34] should be described rather like this: it is marriage that must place itself facing the theological property of virginity in order to understand itself. Let us say — for now — that this was necessarily going to be the case; let us say that it is theologically normal that it happened like this. And this is the primary teaching of the Patristic tradition."[35]

Father Sicari then distances himself from this patristic position by seeking to go beyond the theology of the states of perfection that had been attested, following the Church Fathers, also by the great medieval Doctors of the Church and other writers, right up to the Second Vatican Council. The Carmelite father starts from the premise that the rule of evangelical radicalism is an essential element of Christian novelty, and hence of all the states of life. He then sees a precise alignment between the earlier theology and the desire to revisit the traditional theology of the evangelical counsels in favor of a new theology of "evangelical counsel." By this he means that all Christian existence is in fact a "state of counsel," in other words, a "state of new life."[36]

For Father Sicari, the greatest difficulty to surmount is the consideration that the virginal/celibate state is "a superior state in itself, as the way of perfection required of everyone, but which cannot be adopted by everyone."[37] In other words, a sort of charismatic *aporia*, or ambiguity, which, however, would be overcome if one begins to speak instead of a state of life that God calls a person to rather than a choice made by man. And, indeed, God does call everyone to perfection. Therefore, there would no longer be any difference between the evangelical counsels and marriage since all Christian life would become a "counsel." Anything can then be counseled to actuate full charity without formal obligations, but with the counsel still retaining its binding force.[38]

Father Sicari would thus see "divine jealousy" as the theological explanation for, and distinction between, the theological properties of conjugal love and virginal love,[39] with consecrated virginity no longer having the excellence of serving as a model of the possible embodiment of ultimate perfection in the eyes of God. In this way, the two states of life would no longer be just complementary but also equal, despite the diversity of their gifts.

It is important to also mention the position of Karl Rahner, since he would become a reference point for many.[40] According to the German Jesuit, divine charity becomes redemptive by bursting into the world as an event of grace. Moreover, every event of grace always has two distinctive features: it is an incarnation into the reality that it saves and sanctifies, and at the same time a rupture of that same reality with an eye to the future. In other words, in every event of grace, we distinguish between a moment of incarnation and a moment of eschatology.[41]

While marriage already has a natural dimension that renders it manifest and comprehensible to the eyes of the world, virginity presents itself instead as a new and unfathomable reality that manifests the transcendence of grace and faith. Rahner's viewpoint came to be seen unquestioningly as authoritative, especially at a time when attempts were being made to describe the state of consecrated life mostly as "an eschatological sign," relegating its particular significance to the afterlife, while forgetting that also Christian marriage, being a sacrament, is itself a new reality in rupture with the way of thinking of the world. It is true that in the First Letter to the Corinthians, St. Paul's counsel regarding virginity is inserted in the context of the *parousia* and that "time is now short." It is also true that the Christian is introduced into this eschatological dimension, which does indeed characterize the entire Pauline teaching by means of his Baptism; hence, everyone must remain in the same condition they were in (married or celibate) when called by the Lord (see 1 Cor. 7:20).[42]

With the Resurrection of Christ, all Christian life is already brought to its ultimate moment. Linking the consecrated life exclusively to its ultimate and transcendent significance simply means losing the very meaning of perfection in this world. Marriage, too, risks being squeezed into an excessively worldly notion of evangelical perfection. Either perfection is already available visibly on earth, and more or less fully realizable here according to the degree of spousal love with God, or we risk losing every trace of it. We will return to this topic later.

Another important author on this subject is Hans Urs von Balthasar. In his work *The Christian State of Life*,[43] he chooses to speak of "states of election" when referring *in primis* to the consecrated life and to the ministerial priesthood, including ecclesiastical celibacy. For him, such election is the model of the Christian life and is at the service of the lay state of life, whose most proper manifestation is Matrimony. The state of election and the lay state of life do not compete, nor can they exist without each other, but both are necessary to build the mystical Body of Christ and are hierarchically ordered to one another.

In this regard, we must agree with the objection levelled against the Swiss theologian for his excessive insistence on portraying consecrated life as a representation of the original state of man prior to sin and as "paradigmatic" of the Christian life by virtue of the "renunciation," through the evangelical counsels, after sin entered the world. On the other hand, one cannot easily dismiss his view of the state of election as superior to the lay state in terms of vocational excellence.[44]

It is true that "election" is a term directed to all Christians and refers to predestination in Christ (cf. Eph. 1:4–5), which is why it is useful to resume employing the traditional term "state of perfection," but it is just as true that religious life is superior to lay vocation as the *means* for reaching union with God in charity. The religious state of life is more perfect because it is specifically designed for the accomplishment of exterior acts of perfection that a married lay person is not able to perform. Different is the case of a celibate lay person who lives a life of perfect chastity for the sake of the Kingdom of Heaven.

Of course, religious life is structured on Christ. However, the Lord's celibacy is not simply an example He gives to restore the *ante-peccatum* condition of man, given that the command to increase and multiply was given to Adam and Eve before sin as part of creation (which is why the meaning of von Balthasar's "fecund virginity" of our first parents in the Garden of Eden is very hard to understand).[45] Rather, His celibacy is the manifestation of His being Son of the Father and one with Him (see John 10:30). In turn, Mary's virginal conception by the work of the Holy Spirit attests and reveals the divinity of Christ and His eternal generation from the Father.

The evangelical counsels are not, therefore, the means for re-proposing the lost Eden; rather, they are the instrument for conforming to the lives of Jesus and Mary to manifest the priority of God above all things and to proclaim that union with God in Heaven is already attainable here on earth through the profession of religious vows. Heavenly perfection is not just achievable in the next life or just interiorly but is possible even in this life in a way that, while not fully perfect since not yet consummated, is still superior to that achievable in the lay state.[46]

Religious life is the way of perfection as it is the representation of Jesus's total love for the Father and
of His undivided dedication to preaching the Gospel
of the Kingdom.

Eschatology is always a moment that is *already
present even if not yet realized*. If consecrated life as
the *Christian perfection already present* is done away
with, the *not yet realized* shall drift further and further away from man's horizon. The "eschatological
sign" of religious life becomes possible only if the life
of the Kingdom of Heaven can already be achieved
here on earth.

Nonetheless, there is a question lingering in the
background: Is the religious life, therefore, an antic-
ipation of heavenly life in God's Kingdom? Yes, it is.
However, not in the sense of religious life exhausting
the depths of Christian life to the point of almost
nullifying other forms of life, but in the measure in
which it relives the total consecration of Christ to the
Father through His virginal generation from Mary,
she also being consecrated to God in her perpetual
virginity.

In our view, the question concerning the states
of life should be framed more explicitly around the
notion of "spousal love."[47] The *culmen* of Christian perfection — namely, holiness — is union with
the Lord until becoming one spirit with Him (cf.
1 Cor. 6:17). Now, the most perfect state of life is
that which comes closest to this fullness of union
in love by being unfailingly the means to the end —
namely, one's sanctification and that of others. Each

state of life is in and of itself a means to this end. Only God is an end unto Himself. Hence, there is necessarily a hierarchy of perfection of this spousal love: its natural and sacramental foundation is manifested by spouses in marriage, while the religious manifest its perfection achievable here on earth in this life as the means of union with Christ and as the *sign* of perfect union with Him for all Christians. If the hierarchy of perfection of love is eliminated, then we should conclude that the angels love God less perfectly than men do.

There are not two juxtaposed or even antithetical ways, where the more perfect one — the virginal or celibate — would in practice negate the possibility of perfection in married life. There is only one way, that of charity. It is a matter of growing in charity toward God and toward our neighbor. Precisely because it is about growing in this perfection, it is necessary to establish a hierarchy in this growth. Charity, being the end, does not admit hierarchies within itself, but the states of life, the means ordered toward it, can be more or less perfect. Just as the very beings created by God are more or less perfect (on account of their being analogically more or less close to Him), so too the good acts that a man can perform can be more or less perfect. A good action always involves a degree of perfection as a function of the ones who act, of their motive, of the means they use, and of the ends they aim for. If this hierarchy of perfection is ignored, there is a tendency to level out everything, including perfection itself. Nor does it suffice to put oneself in the place of God making a choice and to see perfection as that unity of all charisms that could overcome the supposed contradiction between perfection being required of all, while in practice being achievable only by a few. However, this would not be sufficient, because while it is God who invites man to be perfect, it is man that must choose to become so. Anyway, if the hierarchy of evangelical perfection in this life is silenced or leveled out, ultimately God Himself, who is its unparalleled summit, will be ignored.

Replacing the hierarchy of perfection with a sort of commonality of perfection leads to the loss of its true finality, which is union with God. Has not something like this happened after the Second Vatican Council? Perfection is found in God, our heavenly Father. But the way to reach it is human, sustained and vivified by grace and the different charisms. Only by establishing the flawless superiority of the charism of virginity for the Kingdom of Heaven can all charisms be held together and unified harmoniously to enrich the fabric of the Church.

The liturgy also provides a testimony of the supremacy of virginity over the married state. The anaphora of St. Basil, in its memento dedicated to the clergy and to all of God's people, commemorates at the altar those living in virginity for their ministries as a distinct category that precedes those of all the other faithful.[48]

Without the religious life — which can also be called rightly and analogically the "angelic life" — one loses the public *sign* of *toto corde* union with God, together with the necessary link between lay life and the contemplation of God in Heaven. The laity without the religious can no longer understand the necessity of becoming *one* with the Lord and how it is possible to achieve union with Him even living in the body while still physically apart from Him. A religious life that does not exercise its characteristic virginal spousal love de facto stifles every yearning of the heart for God, with the risk of ultimately losing its finality and God Himself. Mary's virginity, and therefore also virginity lived as Mary lived it, is the *sign* of God's presence in this world.

NEW DISCIPLES OF JOVINIAN

The attempt to reduce religious life from a state of perfection to something special yet not superior to all other vocations runs parallel to the effort of subordinating virginity to Matrimony. In 1954, Pius XII published the encyclical *Sacra virginitas* to reaffirm the superior value of virginity and of perfect chastity consecrated to the service of God in the Church by placing them among "*the most precious treasures*" that her Author left to her. Among other things, Pius XII lamented, "However, since there are some who, straying from the right path in this matter, so exalt marriage as to rank it ahead of virginity and thus depreciate chastity consecrated to God and clerical celibacy, Our apostolic duty demands that We now declare and uphold the Church's teaching on the sublime state of virginity, and so defend Catholic truth against these errors."[49]

In fact, as the angelic shepherd said, "This doctrine of the excellence of virginity and of celibacy and of their superiority over the married state was, as we have already said, revealed by our divine Redeemer and by the Apostle of the Gentiles; so too, it was solemnly defined as a dogma of divine faith by the holy council of Trent (Sess. XXIV, can. 10: DH 1810) and explained in the same way by all the holy Fathers and Doctors of the Church."[50]

And yet, right up until now there has been an unflagging, relentless effort to try to prove the contrary, with the inevitable consequences of dissolution of Matrimony, ecclesiastical celibacy, and religious life. If the hierarchy — that is to say, the divine order of Christian perfection — is missing, then perfection itself will fade away.

The forefather of these worldly attacks opposing the most perfect good of *Sacra virginitas* was the monk Jovinian, who lived in the early days of Christianity and died in the year 405. St. Jerome flared up against him, confuting his attacks with two books *Contra Iovinianum* written in 392, as did St. Augustine and St. Ambrose. Jovinian had published in Rome a short treatise in Latin (the existence of which is attested to by St. Jerome in his fiery response), wherein he argued, among other things, that a virgin is not better than a married woman because virgins, widows, and married women, while similar in other ways, all have equal merit in the eyes of God, as they have all passed (via Baptism) through the wellspring of Christ. According to him, moreover, those who have been baptized could no longer sin, and eventually, the same reward in the Kingdom of Heaven would be granted to all those who had kept their baptismal promises.

In a nutshell, Jovinian staked everything on Baptism, regarding it superior to all other vocations. However, by reducing Christian perfection to Baptism, the renegade monk lowered the aspiration and intensity of Christian life, and he elevated marriage above virginity, mixing Stoicism (for its belief that there is no difference among sins) with Epicureanism (for its justification of sensual pleasures), as St. Augustine would note in his letter to St. Jerome.[51]

St. Jerome's scorching response was swift in coming. So much so that he was rebuked for disparaging Matrimony in his defense of virginity.[52] On the contrary, the hermit saint had explained very well why virginity is more excellent than Matrimony without, however, disparaging it, even when the honor of the former is preferred to the good of the latter.

Thus writes St. Jerome:

> This circumstance [the rhetorical way in which Jovinian wrote] wisely leads me to suspect that his objective in proclaiming the excellence of matrimony was simply to denigrate virginity. This is because when that which is inferior is placed on the same level of that which is superior, the inferior benefits by virtue of the comparison, but that which is higher suffers detriment.
>
> As far as we are concerned, we are no disciples of Marcion or of Manichæus, who despise marriage. Nor are we deceived by the error of Tatian, the chief

of the Encratites, into supposing all sexual relations unclean. For he condemns and rejects not just marriage, but also the food which God has created for us to enjoy....

But while we honor marriage, we prefer the virginity which springs from it. Will silver stop being silver on account of gold being more precious? Or is it an insult to a tree to prefer its apples to its roots or its leaves? Or is it an injury to grain to put the ear before the stalk and the blade? As apples come from the tree and grain from the straw, so virginity comes from wedlock.[53]

For the Dalmatian saint, continence is not contrary to man's nature but superior to it, perfecting it by elevating it to a higher level through grace. And then, there is his reference to Mary's virginity to finally put Jovinian out of his misery: "'Behold a virgin shall conceive and bear a son' (Isa 7:14). If virginity is not preferable to marriage, why didn't the Holy Ghost choose a married woman or a widow?"[54]

The Virgin Mary is the *form* of virginity in the Church, its exemplary model, and she is the one who guides us in discovering virginity's excellence over marriage so we do not blur the hierarchy of Christian perfection and we avoid making God the common ground of our imperfections and worldly desires.

In 392, Jovinian was condemned in Rome by Pope Siricius, along with eight of his followers. His condemnation was reported also to St. Ambrose, the bishop of Milan, who in 393 ratified the Roman sentence for his diocese and in the same year composed *Exortatio virginitatis*. His spiritual son, St. Augustine, wrote in 401 first his *De bono coniugali* and then his *De sancta virginitate*. Thus, the heresy of the superiority of Matrimony over fruitful virginity for the Kingdom of Heaven seemed to have been well and truly eradicated. On the contrary, and most astonishingly, it has continued to spread and burn like flames under embers, up until the turn of the Second Vatican Council and, we should now say, until the present day.

Indeed, if it is asserted (notwithstanding grueling, hermeneutical debates and lengthy deliberation) that *Amoris laetitia* admits the divorced and remarried to sacramental Communion, overcoming the Church's hitherto praxis (and doctrine), are Jovinian's theses not being reintroduced today? *Mutatis mutandis*, if in fact the divorced and civilly remarried are to be authorized by their confessor to live in a union that is not a real marriage, thus living like husband and wife even though they are not, it is *de facto* affirmed not only that Matrimony is superior to virginity but also, in a yet more epicurean way, that sexual intercourse is superior to both Matrimony and virginity.

Even the stoical perspective is left in the background. An attempt has been made to justify this proposition[55] of *Amoris Laetitia* by invoking the invincible ignorance of the unmarried couple. However, how could one be ignorant about their state of life or justify the confessor's silence about this presumed ignorance regarding such a grave matter? Then there is the supposed need to safeguard a higher value, such as the good of the children, using proportionalist or consequentialist ethics to distinguish between "pre-moral goods" (such as sexual intercourse) and "moral goods" (such as the good of the couple and of the children). In such a situation, sexual relations *more uxorio* (as husband and wife but outside marriage) would remain in principle something to avoid (though obviously no longer something intrinsically evil) but justifiable in its practical dimension. In such a way, praxis prevails over the objectivity of the moral life, dooming the perfection of Christian life to just plodding along: not just in the way Christians are called to choose an inferior good in preference to one that is objectively better — if in fact Matrimony is put on the same level as consecrated life — but also in the way they are permitted to actually choose what is evil instead of what is good. This is the logical consequence of years of doctrinal decline and the pervasiveness of a certain theology of praxis, where distinctions have been cancelled for the sake of the primacy of man. The origin of the decline has a common denominator: the refusal of the primacy and excellence of virginity consecrated to God, at the root of which is undoubtedly the downsizing of Mariology and especially the refusal of the dogma of Mary's perpetual virginity. A truth that has been reinterpreted along the lines of biological categories or reduced for pedagogic reasons to a mere theological narrative.

Lo and behold, today we find ourselves in a Church where Jovinian would be heeded and promoted to the highest levels, whereas St. Jerome, St. Augustine, and

St. Ambrose would be branded as Pharisees. Jovinian sought to convince the "*sanctimoniales*" with theological and moral arguments that maintaining virginity is of no real use because God's recompense is the same for everyone. Hence, it is better to get married rather than miss the opportunity. What is surprising (but perhaps not all that much!) is that Jovinian was a monk. Today, it is supposedly better to live as husband and wife in a *more uxorio* union rather than forgo carnal pleasures. Abstinence is apparently detrimental to the spirit, and in any case, God's mercy is the same for everyone. Both arguments denote the obfuscation of God's primacy and that of union with the Lord until we have become *one* with Him.

These affinities between Jovinian and the present Church are of no small significance, then, urging us to face today the same problem of yesterday: the loss of the supreme good of chaste, virginal love chosen to give witness to God's primacy over everything and everyone. The Church is the virginal bride of the Word of God and the only way to the eschatological Kingdom, where "they shall neither marry nor be married; but shall be as the angels of God in heaven" (Matt. 22:30). We believe that the Church will be able to rise again from the present crisis, which is principally a crisis of identity, by viewing with clear-sighted eyes the good of virginity that, while surpassing marriage as the highest perfection, grounds the latter in its true nature.

We said earlier that the crisis of consecrated life is very similar to the crisis of the sacrament of

Matrimony. They are intertwined. We are firmly convinced of this crisis, and *Amoris laetitia* is clear proof of it. The actual root of our conviction, from which it derives, is in St. Jerome's very poignant verdict: *virginity is the offspring of Matrimony*, deriving from it. If virginity no longer exists, it is because Matrimony has no longer given birth to it. If marriage no longer has its primary end in the generation of children, obviously also perpetual chastity will not be forthcoming, and, vice versa, if chaste and virginal love loses its primacy, Matrimony will lose its fundamental mission, along with its identity, as the cradle of life and the soul of society. Virginity is the foundation of Matrimony, being its most beautiful fruit.[56] Matrimony heralds virginity, being its root. Either virginity and Matrimony remain firmly united and hierarchically ordered or both fall.

Their distinction in the way the lower perfection is subordinated to the higher one is sealed and fulfilled magnificently in the Virgin Mary. It is she to whom we must look to rise again from our existential fall. It is she to whom the Church looks when teaching virginity's superiority over Matrimony. We are certain that a certain disdain for Mariology, along with the neo-Ebionite[57] attempt to dispute our Lady's virginity, have hastened the present deviation in these postconciliar years. Therefore, it is precisely by returning to the Church's authentic and uninterrupted faith in Mary's perpetual virginity that we can seek to respond to the present malaise. We have acclaimed Matrimony and the parity of the states in life to such an extent that we are on the brink of losing both the pearl of virginity and the virtue of Matrimony.

Alongside this malaise, there is also the embarrassment for man and young people of speaking about virginity as a virtue; it seems almost like a taboo to be discarded. Our Lady truly is the answer. The solution is a clear and lively faith in our Lady's perpetual virginity. The *Semper Virgo* is Christianity's necessary hermeneutical key, especially with regards to the Kingdom of Heaven. Christ enters the world only through Mary, by the gate of her virginity. This is precisely the truth that we want to shed light on to find our way out of the *impasse* that is gripping us. We need to rediscover the *form*.

CHAPTER 2

Mary's Virginity
Is the Christian Form

*"Rubum quem viderat Moyses incombustum
conservatam agnovimus tuam laudabilem
virginitatem: Dei genitrix, intercede pro nobis"*[58]

ARRIAGE AND VIR-
ginity must once again find
their harmony in the footsteps
of Christ and His Gospel. They must shine in their
complementarity. As already mentioned, this cannot happen when the two vocations are considered
uniform, or the same, but in the coming together
of their individual uniqueness, urged on by the *car-
itas Christi*. In order for this harmony to take place,
the two vocations must be united not at the lowest
level, in a horizontal way, but at the highest level; it is
vital that they find this concord not in themselves (*in
se*) but in something else (*in alio*), in a mystery that
precedes both marriage and consecrated virginity, a
mystery that while establishing each of them in their
distinctive, charismatic character, goes beyond them
in a transcendent and definitive realm.

Marriage and virginity can be mutually beneficial if
both are in harmony with Mary's virginity, and precisely by virtue of this bond, they can find their dis-
tinctiveness and the hierarchy necessary to safeguard

God's primacy above all things, the primacy of He who is Spirit (cf. John 4:24). Mary's virginity says to man that virginity/celibacy is the more excellent state of life since it is intimately connected to God's eternity and, at the same time, that marriage can in no wise be debased since it offers the natural and sacramental foundation of spousal love, which grows and perfects itself in the measure in which it reaches union with God.

On this ladder reaching up to Heaven there is a place for the various Christian vocations and for the different states of life. This is the very ladder that connects Heaven and earth, given that it soars vertically above the things of man, carrying them upwards to God. In this ladder, we can recognize Mary's virginity. No wonder that the Virgin is acclaimed in the Byzantine hymn *Akathistos* (fifth and sixth centuries) as the "celestial ladder" who brought God among men, as the "bridge" who brings men to Heaven, and as the "gateway" to the sacred mystery.[59] However, Mary's holy virginity will be able to serve in the Church as the "ladder" that raises men heavenwards only if it is also recognized as the "form" of Christian life, as the most perfect "type" and principle that bestows perfection to things, since it confers to them their being. The Virgin Mary is the form that shapes Christian being. Let us proceed step by step, however, as we try to examine this aspect in more detail.

In the first place, we should ask ourselves what we mean by "form." Let us consider this term in its original and metaphysical meaning, singularly assigned to it by Aristotle, who, out of all the ancient philosophers, knew best how to determine its precise significance. For Aristotle, *form* is primarily the principle that determines the essence of matter, conferring to it its perfection. *Form* relates to the structure of being. In order *to be*, and therefore *to be in a particular way*, an entity must receive *being*. In this case, the *form* is also the act of being. For this reason, Aristotle defines the *form* as the cause of things and as the quintessential "species" because it specifies the things that are,[60] conferring to them their primary perfection, which is indeed their being. (At the metaphysical level, a *form* corresponds to a specific difference at the logical level.) The *form* allows things to move from the state of potentiality to that of actuality—namely, from the pure possibility of being to the actual act of existing.[61] According to Aristotle, existence, which is the "species" of being in a metaphysical sense, is, consequently, also the first and ultimate perfection of being. It is infused into another thing by an agent that actually possesses it, and which is the end itself of its own action;[62] while, to be clear, the *form*, once so participated, is and stays in things instead of remaining, as Plato wanted, in the *hyperuranion*, the Platonic realm of separate ideas.[63]

We now wish to capture the essence of this *form*, understood in the metaphysical and primarily Aristotelian sense, and transfer it analogically to the Blessed Virgin Mary—and specifically, to her virginity, as the initial and final cause of being Christian. Mary's virginity is the Christian *form* because it acts as the structural perfection of Christian life. It is the original and

definitive perfection, the beginning but also the fulfillment of the Kingdom of Heaven. It is the *beginning*
because Mary's perpetual virginity is the expression
of her being the immaculate creation *of* God without
stain and corruption, as well as the immaculate creation
for God so He can become flesh and dwell among us.
The virginity of Mary is the being of God with us. It is
the *fulfillment* because it signifies the way of being in
God forever, in an eternity of heavenly contemplation.
It is the finality of a love that does not dissipate, does
not change, and does not perish.

Moreover, Mary's virginity is the *form* of Christianity because it is the womb that forges all vocations,
giving them their unity and hierarchical distinction.
With Mary, there is no kind of careerism in holiness;
one does not get sidetracked by the ambiguity of a
perfection required by all (or universal holiness) but
realized only by those readily labeled as predestined or
pure. With Our Lady, everyone is invited to come to
the height of holiness. With her, one does not fall into
some kind of gnostic Catharism, which is the heresy
that condemned the flesh and matter but embracing
in fact perversions against nature. Marriages are holy
because they are purified by the virginal Blood of Jesus
and of His Mother. Precisely for this reason, they must
not be transformed into mere self-interest in search of
pleasure for its own sake. Likewise, virginity does not
become the narcissism of perfection, since it is the gift
of one's own body as a holy oblation offered to enable
everyone in the Church, mainly the married, to learn
how to offer themselves by donating their own bodies,

bodies that become the body of Christ and the temple of the Holy Spirit. Christ is the end of all things, and everything converges in Him through the virginal purity of His Mother, the sacred crucible that purifies everything, raising it to the throne of God. Mary's virginal womb gives form to Christian life, bestowing it with its harmonious synthesis of all the charisms lived out with a view to sanctity. Only by power of our Lady's most pure virginity, which anticipates the Church, imparting fruition to her in Heaven, can all vocations and states of life find their proper place and the authentic synergy for everyone's sanctification.

We feel the need for a *form* especially today, at a time of "heresy of formlessness" (or, as in the original term, of "loss of form," *Formlosigkeit*), as the German writer Martin Mosebach would say[64] — a heresy that threatens *in primis* the liturgy in the devastation of its rite, of the sacred as such, and of the capacity of prayer to be raised up to God rather than remaining an expression of human chatter. This is a common heresy that threatens the perennial doctrinal expression of the Faith, impacting Christian morality and spirituality, which these days are dissipated into pastoral formulas devoid of form and focus.

A sort of amorphism prevails when the differences between the states of life are compressed and conflated into the notion of perfection, without realizing, however, that perfection is the *aim* of all states of life rather than being their common element. Merely because all states of life tend to perfection does not mean that they are equal but simply that perfection is possible in any one of them. Such deviation from steadfast theological development produces Christian "amorphism." When everything is the same, then everything is also taken for granted. Is it just a coincidence that nowadays there is a tendency to no longer canonize those who actually lived a distinguished life of heroic virtue, favoring instead those who distinguished themselves by merely historical acts deemed to have been heroic? Mary's virginity is the Christian *form* since it is the quintessential "species" that throughout history reminds us of *what Christianity actually is*. When a child allows himself to be formed by his Mother, and consciously welcomes this maternal form, then Mary's heart opens to him and *already* anticipates in that moment the new heavens and new earth to come. The *already* of Mary foreshadows *the not yet* of all her children.

Moreover, Mary is the *form* of Christianity because, as St. Augustine says, Christ took his "human form" from her, through the work of the Blessed Trinity,[65] so that *"from her salvation was born for us among men."*[66] She is the disciple par excellence even prior to, and far more than, being the Mother of Christ. She is just like an initiation to discipleship and the exemplary model for Christ's disciples.

As St. Augustine of Hippo bluntly tells us, "Did not the Virgin Mary do the will of the Father? I mean, she believed by faith, she conceived by faith, she was chosen to be the one from whom salvation in the very midst of the human race would be born for us, she was created by Christ before Christ was created in her. Yes, of course, holy Mary did the will of the Father. And therefore, it means more for Mary to have been a disciple of Christ than to have been the mother of Christ."[67]

The Virgin Mary is "Christ-shaped," modeled on Christ, so she can be the "Christ-former," or even the "Christ-maker," for Jesus's disciples. This notion is very dear to Father Stefano M. Manelli, who, in his spiritual wisdom, writes, "Having been willed and formed...as 'forma Christi,'[68] it is quite logical to say that Our Blessed Lady was directly and precisely made 'Christ-shaped' to be, indeed, the 'Christ-former,' or even the 'Christ-maker,' foremostly for Christ, the Head of the mystical Body; but also in Him, for all the redeemed who, responding to the call for holiness, must and desire to become 'Christ-formed,' as true 'brothers' of Jesus, of He who is, indeed, 'the first-born of many brothers' (Rm 8:29), all of them children of the Virgin Mary."[69]

It is interesting to note that among the oldest formularies of Marian litanies, originating in the twelfth century,[70] there appears also the invocation *Forma sanctitatis*.[71] Mary is the form of Christian holiness because she herself, *in primis*, is all holy.

The theology of the Virgin Mary as the form of Christ and of Christians resonates deeply in the liturgy. The liturgy of Christmastide expresses in a unique way the importance of Mary's "fecund virginity," which becomes the instrument of salvation for all mankind.

In the Christmas Vespers, the Church sings the hymn *Jesu Redemptor omnium*, which in the third verse mentions Mary's virginal womb as the *form* of Christ's body, in accordance with our body. Here it is in the original Latin, followed by my translation.[72]

Memento, rerum Conditor,
Nostri quod olim corporis,
Sacrata ab alvo Virginis
Nascendo formam sumpseris.

Remember, O Creator of the world,
that Thou didst assume the form of our body,
by being born of the sacred womb of a Virgin.

The prayer for the Octave of the Nativity of the Lord, prayed in the liturgy of Compline from December 24 onwards, praises Mary's fecund virginity. The text is a veritable compendium of the theology of Mary's virginity. Mary, as virgin in a perpetual and fruitful way — or in a fruitfully perpetual way — is the mediatrix of the grace of salvation for the entire human race. Her virginity is the seal on God's *fiat* to Man.

Here is the original followed by my translation:[73]

Deus, qui salutis aeternae, beatae Mariae virginitate
fecunda, humano generi praemia praestitisti: tribue,
quaesumus; ut ipsam pro nobis intercedere sentia-
mus, per quam meruimus auctorem vitæ suscipere,
Dominum nostrum Iesum Christum Filium tuum.

O God, who by the fruitful virginity of Blessed Mary,
have brought forth to mankind the reward of eternal
salvation grant, we beseech You, that we may experi-
ence the intercession of she, through whom we merited
to receive the Author of Life, Your Son, Our Lord
Jesus Christ.

THE FORM THAT UNITES
VIRGINITY AND SPOUSAL LOVE

Mary's virginity is the "spousal thalamus" ("nuptial-chamber" or "bridal-chamber") from which Christ comes forth to unite to Himself (in His body taken from the Virgin) His mystical Body, the Church. Mary's virginity gives birth to Christ and thus gives form to the Church. Mary is the *type* among virgins that remain virgin in their body and of all those who, as Christ's members, must remain virgin in spirit. This is a notion dear to the Fathers, especially to the great St. Augustine, who guides us with an illuminating sermon on the Lord's Nativity.

St. Augustine first addresses the unbelievers in Christ's divinity by referencing two intimately connected miracles — namely, the body of the resurrected Christ appearing in the Cenacle behind locked doors and that same body coming forth "like a bridegroom from his nuptial-chamber, which is to say from the virginal womb, leaving His Mother's integrity inviolate."[74] In fact, according to St. Augustine, "the more the faith acknowledges them both, the more incredulity rejects them both."[75] St. Augustine then goes on to illustrate the grace of Christmas. The Word, by uniting human nature to Himself in Mary's virginal nuptial-chamber, united the virginal, chaste Church to Himself so that everyone, whether virgin or not, may possess an untainted heart. All are betrothed to the one bridegroom, and virgins are the emblem of this because, in celebrating the Virgin's birth, they can exult in the fact that they have been born from the untainted virginity of the Church through Baptism. Thus, the holy bishop of Tagaste writes:

The only begotten Son of God deigned to take upon himself a human nature drawn from a virgin so that he might thus link a spotless Church to himself, its spotless founder. In doing so he not only thought of virgins undefiled in body, but he also desired that, in that Church which the Apostle Paul calls a virgin, the minds of all should be undefiled. "For I betrothed you to one spouse, that I might present you a chaste virgin to Christ."

The Church, therefore, imitating the Mother of her Lord in mind, though not in body, is both mother and virgin. Since the virginity of his Mother was in no way violated in the birth of Christ, He likewise made His Church a virgin by ransoming her from the fornication of demons. You holy virgins, born of her undefiled virginity, who, scorning earthly nuptials, have chosen to be virgins in the flesh, rejoice now and celebrate with all solemnity the fecundity of the Virgin on this day. The Lord was, indeed, born of a woman, but He was conceived in her without man's co-operation. He who has offered to you this blessing of virginity to cherish did not deprive His Mother of that gift. Far be it that He who repairs in you the harm wrought by Eve should even in the slightest degree mar in His Mother Mary that virginity which you have prized.[76]

At the end of his sermon, after highly praising the virgins beloved by Christ, as His Mother was, St. Augustine addresses everyone present with the exhortation that that which is in the body of Mary, her spousal virginity, may dwell in the soul of every Christian: "Finally, I address all here present; I speak to all; I include in my exhortations the whole Church, that chaste virgin whom the Apostle speaks of as espoused to Christ. Do, in the inner chambers of your soul, what you view with amazement in the flesh of Mary. He who believes in his heart unto justice conceives Christ; he who with his mouth makes profession of faith unto salvation brings forth Christ. Thus, in your souls, let fertility abound and virginity be preserved."[77]

In this setting, Mary's spousal bond with Christ by virtue of her virginity, the nuptial-chamber where the Word takes on our flesh, is very clear. Her womb prepares the birth of the Church, bride of Christ, where all souls are promised to the one bridegroom, and they themselves promise their fidelity to Christ in the virginal chastity of the Church. All souls, all of Christ's members, participate therefore in a virginal chastity, which the Church is rich in because she imitates the Virgin Mary by becoming, like her, virgin for her exclusive love of Christ and mother for her capacity to generate men to God.[78] Mary's virginity, then, acts as the spousal vessel of the Church to Christ. This is possible as, *in primis*, it is the Virgin Mary who has united herself to the Son through a virginal marriage.

Mary is Christ's bride, and that is precisely how she unites the Church to Christ in a spousal way. This is another notion dear to the Church Fathers. Alongside Augustine's image of the nuptial-chamber that is Mary's virginal womb, we find the spousal theology of St. Maximus the Confessor in the Byzantine Church. Commenting on the mystery of the

Annunciation, he attributes to the Holy Spirit Mary's adornment as bride of the Lord, who becomes incarnate in her. St. Maximus addresses Mary, recalling what the angel says to her: "The Holy Ghost shall come upon thee, and the power of the most High shall overshadow thee" (Luke 1:35) to "prepare and adorn you as the bride worthy of the Lord, and to sanctify from the beginning your holy body and soul adorned with godly virtues. And immediately your immortal bridegroom and Son, who is the power of the Most High, will overshadow you, for Christ is the power of God and the wisdom of God."[79]

Christ is both spouse and son of Mary. The spousal love of the Mother is inseparable from her virginity. And it is precisely this reality that resonates in the most ancient Marian hymn of the Byzantine Church, the *Akathistos*[80] (fifth to sixth century). Each of the twenty-four verses that comprise it (as well as the initial troparion and *kontàkion*) closes with a chorus that praises Mary as "O Bride unwedded," meaning "Virgin and Bride."[81]

Returning to the West, the first among the Latin Fathers to speak of Mary's spousal love with God,[82] in reference to the Son who becomes incarnate in her, is St. Peter Chrysologous (ca. 380–450), bishop of Ravenna, at that time capital of the western part of the Roman Empire. In commenting on the mystery of the Annunciation, where Mary, by then already Joseph's bride, is presented by the Evangelist as "the virgin," he fashions a magnificent reference to her as bride of God, not taken away from Joseph but simply returned to Christ to prepare for the spousal love between creature and Christ in His mystical Body.

Thus writes the holy bishop of Ravenna, "Swiftly does this ambassador [Gabriel] fly to the bride, that he may assert God's claim to her as His own. Gabriel takes her not from Joseph, but he restores her to Christ, to whom she was espoused when she was first formed in the womb. Christ, therefore, did but take His own when He thus made Mary His bride. It is not a separation that He thus produces, but a union with Himself of His own creature by becoming incarnate in her womb."[83]

This is all about Mary's divine marriage to her divine Son. Thus, through Christ, Mary will be able to take part in the spousal love with the most Holy Trinity. It seems clear from this patristic reading that Mary's spousal love with God has, in her spousal relationship with Christ,[84] the principal analogue which subsequently extends also to the Holy Spirit and the Father.

Mary unites virginity and spousal love, epitomizing them in her union with Christ. To use another typology dear to the Fathers, she is the New Eve at the side of the New Adam. Virginity leads to spousal love and spousal love, in turn, must always remain anchored to virginity in all the various states of Christian life, and always aiming towards it, even when it is expressed in married love. Spousal love is always the virginity of love, both when it is fulfilled in the physical intactness of renouncing marriage and in priestly celibacy and when it is experienced in marriage as chastity — namely, as the truth of indissoluble and fruitful love.[85]

The Virgin Mary is, therefore, once again, the form of Christian life because she expresses in her being both virginity and spousal love, showing them to be interdependent. Virginity is fulfilled in spousal love, and spousal love draws its truth from remaining anchored in virginity. The Church sees in Mary a unity of all the diverse states of life of her children, enveloping them in this spousal love, which is ever more perfect the more one is closer to that of the Virgin Mary, in her and for her, and then to that of Christ Himself.

THE FORM THAT UNITES VIRGINITY AND MARTYRDOM

There is another pairing that emerges from a concise analysis of early Christianity. The praise of virginity, which St. Paul and both Eastern and Western Fathers extol in a special way, goes hand in hand with that of martyrdom. The pairing of virginity and martyrdom expresses the intimate bond between purity and a fragrant offering to the point of complete self-donation, a gift ushered in by virginity and fulfilled by martyrdom. Thus, purity and sacrifice become intertwined to the point of sealing into a sacrificial offering the supreme act of charity, which is spousal love, or spousal union. Spousal love and martyrdom are made one. It really does seem that they are made for each other.

This emerges, for example, in St. Ambrose's praise of the martyr St. Agnes in a homily that the saintly bishop of Milan delivered on January 21, St. Agnes's *dies natalis*, and which then goes on to serve as the exordium of a book he dedicates to virgins. Agnes is preparing for martyrdom as if she is going to a wedding.[86] The *virgo* Agnes wants to be *sponsa Christi* forever. St. Ambrose says, "Today is the birthday of a virgin; let us imitate her purity. It is the birthday of a martyr; let us offer ourselves in sacrifice."[87] St. Agnes, whose name is an *omen* (from *agna, agnella,* "sacrificial victim"; while in Greek, from *agne,* "chaste"), offers the *exemplum* of Christ's love. She becomes *example* of intactness and immolation, as a host for Christ, and like Christ. St. Ambrose goes on to say, "The name of the virgin is the title of modesty. I will call her martyr and proclaim her virgin."[88] And then, in an abundance of inspiring details, St. Ambrose describes the union, within Agnes the martyr, of the spouse who sets off for her nuptial-chamber and the virgin who runs in haste to the place of her martyrdom. The bridal-chamber of the virginal nuptials will become scarlet with the blood of this little lamb of Christ. This martyr of just twelve years of age hastens to her nuptial-chamber, which becomes the altar of her sacrifice.

Thus writes St. Ambrose, "A bride would never hasten to her nuptials with so glad a heart, or so light a step, as this young virgin marches to the place of execution. She is decked not with the blithesome show of plaited tresses, but with Christ; she is wreathed not with flowers, but with purity. All stood weeping; Agnes shed not a tear."[89]

The virginal offering and the supreme witness in the martyrdom of blood are fused into a spiritual sacrifice that fulfills the words of the Apostle Paul to the Romans: "Present your bodies a living sacrifice, holy, pleasing unto God" (Rom. 12:1). To the point that Origen shall proclaim, "It would seem therefore that an undefiled body is the living, sacred victim most pleasing to God."[90]

Virginity and spousal love are now welded together in the ultimate witness of a cruel and bloody martyrdom. With Christ's entry into the world, hate and persecution are never far behind. Those who wish to be His followers must be prepared to be put to the test and to suffer. Taking a short step back, what is even more astonishing is how the persecution of the Little Innocents begins immediately after the birth of Jesus. They, without a word passing their lips, are already confessing Christ with their deaths. They are slain out of hatred for Christ and thus are His witnesses. Even in the silent testimony of these defenseless little ones, innocence and virginal candor shine as elements in common with the martyrdom of St. Agnes and of many other holy virgins. These infants who die defenseless are in fact those that follow the Lamb wherever He goes because they are virgins and have not tainted themselves with women (cf. Apoc. 14:4). The liturgy of the Holy Innocents, celebrated on December 28, mindful of Apocalypse 14:4, speaks of the supreme testimony of those children who were able to hide Christ from Herod.[91] They die for Him and are His forever.

Virginity and martyrdom, intertwined in virginal spousal love, characterize the beginnings of Christianity. With the conquest of the Roman Empire to Christ, this bloody martyrdom, this supreme love for Christ all the way up to self-immolation, will be lived out in an unbloody manner in the monastic life consecrated to God. Origen — considered by some as the precursor of monastic life[92] — wished to die a martyr's death and would come to understand that there is also another martyrdom one can undergo for the Lord, which he defines as of the "heart" and of the "conscience."[93] Thus, one slowly moves from the inseparable combination of "virginity and spousal love," which is the primordial form, to that of "virginity and martyrdom," the perfective and definitive form.

In the spousal love with Christ, which began and was lived out in Mary's virginity, everyone in the Church is called to give witness to the Lord of their belonging to Christ by becoming a "host of love," a sacrifice for God and for the brethren. Once again, we have the first-ever form that constitutes what it is to be a Christian, and this can only derive from the *type* of virginal spousal love offered by the Virgin Mary. We could certainly see Mary, *Virgo et Sponsa*, as an *exemplum* of virginal-spousal love in martyrdom, which precedes that of St. Agnes and the other virgin saints because it is the model for the entire Church. This presupposes that we speak of Mary as true co-operatrix in our salvation, as the New Eve alongside Christ as the New Adam,[94] offering herself on Calvary, as icon and Queen of martyrs—in short: Mary as the *Co-Redemptrix* of humanity.[95]

In Mary and in her being Christ's virginal spouse, we also have the beginning of martyrdom as the definitive witness to the Lord. The first and most cruel martyrdom was indeed experienced by her when, standing straight at the foot of the Cross, she sacrificed her Son for all of us and, with Him, sacrificed herself for our salvation—as martyr of love, and sorrow, until the complete consummation of herself with Jesus, and of Jesus in Her, for all of us. Christian life will forever be inscribed with this inseparable duality: virginal and martyrial spousal love as the supreme holocaust of love. Only by uniting both these elements of being with, and for, Christ can each person truly and fully live out the Christian life, according to his or her state in life, and in a measure of love that can grow day after day.

For this reason, an *exemplary model* was desperately needed to enable the development of Christian perfection as lived out by countless saints and disciples of the Lord. A *form* was impressed on Christianity from its very first appearance in the world with the birth of our Lord, and that *form* was immediately discernible in the virginal and sacrificial womb of our Lady, her spousal nuptial-chamber. In her, spousal love becomes sacrificial love. Religious life can once again recover its essence by rediscovering the preciousness of an oblative spirituality, which places the gift of self at its center, to the point of complete self-sacrifice and even martyrdom, while marriage can rely on the indissolubility of chaste and fruitful love.

If our Lady is placed once again at the center, everything can flourish once more because the proper *form* of all things will be restored. She is the original *type* that must be preserved to stop paying the high price of a silent and inevitable collapse into a deformed and sacrilegious amorphism of principles and life. The Virgin Mary is the Church's *type*[96] because she is her icon and exemplary model; she is Christianity's *form* because she is its special distinction and essential perfection. More must be done to recover this *form*.

CHAPTER 3

Virgin Before, During, and after the Birth

"Ave Maria stella,
Dei Mater alma,
atque semper Virgo
Felix caeli porta"[97]

MARY'S VIRGINITY CALLED INTO QUESTION

*M*ARY'S VIRGINITY—succinctly defined as "perpetual," comprising her *virginitas* before, during, and after parturition—is a great *sign*, a sign given by God. Indeed, Isaiah's messianic prophecy (7:14), "Behold a virgin shall conceive and bear a son, and his name shall be called Emmanuel," interprets the mystery of Mary's perpetual virginity as an event that becomes the *sign* of God. Matthew (1:23), recalling Isaiah's text, confirms its prophetic-messianic significance. Mary's intact virginity is the sign of God entering the world. The Emmanuel is the Son of the Perpetual Virgin.

Nowadays, we are witnessing, as we said, a new Ebionite attempt to dilute the dogmatic message and meaning of virginity, most of all the *virginitas in partu*;[98] this attempt involves either ascribing a natural cause to the generation of Jesus or characterizing virginity as unrelated to physiology. Yes, we are told that Mary is a virgin, but not in the sense of her physical intactness consisting in the absence of labor pains and birth-related physico-structural wounds. In this way, virginity is placed into a purely moral and symbolic realm; otherwise, how could we possibly handle the worldly desecrations of physical virginity? Our Lady can then appear to be just a mother like any other mother.

In modern times, Karl Rahner's stance in his dialogue with Mitterer appears emblematic. To find any kind of pretext when speaking with the Viennese doctor, the German Jesuit has no hesitation in jettisoning the truth coming from the *auditus fidei* of the Church rather than from his own theology. In 1952, Albert Mitterer, a priest-physician and specialist in the biological sciences, published a work on the dogma and biology of the Holy Family of Nazareth.[99] In it he sustained, against the common view of the Church Fathers and Doctors, that Mary experienced both the rupture of her physical integrity (the rupture of the hymen) and the pains of labor, and that these, while not necessary for her perfect virginity, were necessary for her perfect maternity. According to the Viennese priest, the disruption of physical integrity resulting from the sexual act would undermine perfect virginity but would nevertheless be necessary to guarantee Mary's perfect maternity.

In this way, our Lady's virginity and maternity were set against each other and lowered to the status of the ordinary, thus removing the possibility of there being an intervention by God beyond the realm of biological science. Physical virginity would then start to be seen in the context of a "symbol," with no connection to reality, thereby becoming an "issue" for theology. Rahner, in his dialogue with the world, did not miss the opportunity to approve Mitterer's thesis, asserting that Mary's virginity in childbirth has no sound foundation.[100]

In fact, the faith of the Church has a vastly different outlook on virginity, not just from a moral perspective, but also, even prior to that, in relation to its physico-structural aspect. Since its very beginning, tradition has made its voice heard on this issue, with St. Ignatius of Antioch declaring that Christ "was in actual fact born of a virgin."[101] Pope Martin I (649–653/5) decided, subsequently, to extend the canons of the Lateran Council of 649 to the entire Church. The third canon, when referring to the conception and the birth, expressly emphasizes the absence of corruption, and thereby Mary's intact virginity, even after the birth.[102]

What is happening today is the rejection of physical reality to seek refuge in more spiritual musings. Ultimately, it amounts to the repudiation of the body and of the true scope of sexuality, to become once again Gnostic and Manichean, propounding every possible aberration against the body so long as the spirit remains unaffected.

No less importantly, the film *Nativity*, directed by Catherine Hardwicke (2006), while accurate and fairly faithful to the details and message of the Gospels on our Lord's Infancy, on the *virginitas in partu* favors certain modern exegetical views over the reality of the two-thousand-year faith of the Church by showing our Lady experiencing labor pains when giving birth to Jesus. As Mike Rich explains, in planning the scene, they were inspired by the book entitled *The Birth of the Messiah*[103] by the renowned American scholar Raymond E. Brown. Obviously, from this point onwards, our criticism is directed more to the scholar than the film, as the latter did nothing more than translate the contents of the book into imagery.

It is then appropriate to understand Brown's position on the virgin birth. In the first place, Brown raises serious doubts about the historical authenticity of Mary's virginal conception. In his view, the biblical testimonies that can be scientifically inspected leave the question of its historical authenticity unresolved;[104] in any case, he says that the virginal conception should be seen not as a myth but rather as the author's literary device that allows him to transition from the Old Testament to the Gospels.

As regards our theme, Brown states, "The fact that Mary herself (instead of the father or the midwife) had wrapped the child [in swaddling clothes], cannot be applied as proof of a miraculous, painless birth, even if the thesis of a miraculous birth rapidly made its appearance in Christian Tradition, as the Protoevangelium 18–19 of James testifies."[105]

In fact, this is not just about the testimony of the *Protoevangelium* of James. Next to it we must also place that of St. Jerome, who saw in the swaddling clothes that the Mother wrapped her Son in the sign of her virginity at the time of the birth.[106]

Concerning the absence of fatigue after the birth as proof of Mary's virginity, we also find St. Maximus the Confessor, who writes, "No ordinary birth pain and suffering appeared in her; on the contrary, she was radiant and extremely beautiful after the birth, as she was also filled with grace and the light of the birth, and this was a marvelous thing for all those who beheld it."[107]

In any case, what Brown relies on is the impossibility of verifying the historicity of Mary's virginity. If there are serious doubts about the virginal conception, there will be even more reasons to then doubt the virginal birth, of which there is no mention, *expressis verbis*, in the Gospels. We find ourselves faced with a historical-critical exegesis that casts aside Church tradition, as if the exegete and the believer were like two dear friends who meet up once in a while.

On many occasions, the exegetical *gambit* of Brown relies on the overtures of the Pontifical Biblical Commission (PBC). Equal status is often unduly attached to the PBC and the Catholic Church on biblical matters, as if the PBC was the supreme Magisterium of the Church.

For Brown, the infancy accounts, when taken together, are a theological instrument for the evangelists rather than historical accounts and, therefore, true. According to Brown, the divine sonship of Jesus in His public ministry enabled Matthew and Luke to look retrospectively at His virginal conception. Moreover, for Brown, exegesis cannot be informed by theological reasoning. In this way, he can easily dismiss the fact that labor pains and physical birth lesions are the result of original sin and that our Lady, being immaculate, could not have suffered such consequences.

For Brown, not even the dogmatic truth of divine biblical inspiration could be taken as proof of the historicity of Mary's virginity. This can only be true up to a point. Certainly, the fact that a book is inspired does not in itself make it historical. In Scripture, there are diverse literary genres. The narrative genre is different from the historical one. However, even the narrative genre, by the very fact that it is inspired, is *true* and not merely literary or theological. Whatever is inspired is true, meaning it actually happened, regardless of how the authors wrote about it. Now, if Luke and Mathew *agree* in saying that Jesus is the virginal son of Mary, conceived by the power of the Holy Spirit, it is contradictory to deny this truth simply under the belief that the accounts are not historical. Luke and Matthew state this explicitly, which means it is either true or historical in the sense intended by Brown. Even if there are only two testimonies, they cannot be simply dismissed. The Fathers professed their faith in the integral virginity of Mary precisely considering these two texts, interpreted within the entire framework of biblical Revelation, as they also did with regards to the *virginitas in partu*.[108]

More recently, another writer has tried to dismantle the truth of the virgin birth with some improbable speculation. In 2006, Andrew Welburn, after studying the Dead Sea Scrolls and other ancient documents for many years, concluded that Matthew's Gospel originates from a Christian-Jewish *background*. Supposedly, Matthew would have had contacts with Jewish sects, such as the Essenes, who we now know had produced a considerable number of scrolls.[109] His account of the birth and childhood of Jesus could have easily developed among these sects, also because by then their ideas had become popularized in the form of romanticized accounts — such as, for example, the story of *Joseph and Aseneth* and the *Apocalypse of Adam*, which shows how the expectation of the Messiah was linked to the idea of a universal revelation through which hope and wisdom are given to the Gentiles. Among these accounts, there is also the gnostic writing titled *The Gospel of Philip*, which would have had a determining role given that it too refers to a virgin birth.

Welburn's effort to find an explanation of a birth that savors of the "miraculous," but from which historical truth must be excluded, is indeed striking. Matthew could certainly have had contacts with the Jewish sects accustomed to apocryphal parabiblical material, yet such association has never been proved; it is a methodological supposition with a strong gnostic inclination.[110] In reality, the unity of Scriptures and oral tradition favoring Christ's virginal birth turns out to be much more logical and self-evident.

And it is decidedly beside the point to refer to Freud's psychoanalysis to place promiscuity and virginity on the same level, as if in a *liminal stage*, so as to view them as complementary and, thereby, rationalize the "myth of the Mother of the Messiah." In fact, this is what the Israeli writer Kara-Ivanov Kaniel has attempted to do recently.[111] What is irksome — today as much as in the past — is for a mother to be a virgin and for a virgin to become a mother. But it is precisely on this very point that the uniqueness of Christianity depends, so long, however, as it is not explained away with some kind of gnostic solution.

"BEHOLD A VIRGIN SHALL CONCEIVE AND BEAR A SON" (IS. 7:14)

In this title, we have referenced Isaiah's prophecy regarding the Virgin Mother. The sign that God will give to King Ahaz and to all the people of Israel — when later with Christianity the doors will be opened to universal salvation for all humanity — will not be a military miracle from the Lord of Hosts, a miracle that can wipe out Israel's enemies, regardless of the whims of those who rely only on men (see Is. 7:11–13); instead, it will be a miracle of a different kind, the sign of a Mother's virginity, of her who is a mother because she is a virgin, and a virgin because she is a mother. It will therefore prove to be an even more astounding miracle; it will be completely unexpected and will thus be a powerful sign — a sign that is beyond human power, which is why it is a sign of God, a miracle of the Most High.[112]

Mary's virginity is the sign of God's presence in history. How can we know that God is with us? Through the sign of the Ever-Virgin Mother (see Is. 7:14; Matt. 1:22–23).

St. Augustine refers convincingly to the mystery of Mary's virginity as "proof" of God's omnipotence and of Christ's divinity:

> In fact, His Virgin Mother has given testimony to His majesty in that she, a virgin before His conception, remained a virgin after childbirth; found with child, she was not made so by man; pregnant with man without man's cooperation, she was more blessed and marvelous in that her fecundity was granted without loss of integrity. People prefer to consider so tremendous a miracle as fictional rather than factual. And the same regarding Christ, the God-Man, since they cannot believe His human attributes, they despise them; since they cannot despise His divine attributes, they do not believe them. However, in proportion as the body of the God-Man in His humiliation is the more abject in their estimation, to that same degree it becomes more pleasing to us; and in proportion as the fruitfulness of a virgin in the birth of a child is more impossible in their eyes, in ours it becomes the more divine.[113]

God is *with* us *in* Mary's virginity. God is *for* us *through* Mary's flawless virginity. It was necessary for the Mother of God to be ever-virgin so that men could recognize in Jesus the Father's only begotten Son, He who is forever generated by the Father: from the Father, He proceeds as the eternal Word, and from Him, He proceeds in His incarnation in Mary's womb as the unfolding mystery of virginal generation. Jesus always *faces* the Father's bosom as the Word (see John 1:18), while He *faces* His Mother's bosom as a man (cf. Luke 1:35).

This is the reason St. John, unlike the synoptic Gospel authors, never refers to Joseph as the "father of Jesus." It is always other people who attribute Joseph's paternity to Jesus (this attribution occurs in John 1:45). Jesus is the only begotten Son of the Father who becomes man without the concourse of man. In Him shines the Father's face (cf. John 14:9); He is the "icon of the invisible God" (Col. 1:15). St. John knows that Jesus's Father is God (see 3:16; 20:31), and he knows that Mary is "the mother of Jesus" (2:1; see also 2:3; 19:25–26). De la Potterie writes, "The fact that Jesus was generated by God Himself was a *sign* and an invitation to men, so that they would recognize in Him the Only Begotten Son of God."[114]

Could the modern difficulty in acknowledging Jesus as the only begotten Son of God, equal to the Father, stem from having reduced Mary's virginity to the pious, compositional ploy of the historian, if not to a mere theological opinion or narrative form — that is, to an invention? Rendering banal this truth of the Faith leads to widespread devastation within the Faith as a whole — a devastation that is even more profound since Mary's virginity is the *sign* of God with us.

The common propensity to opt for a spiritual virginity of Mary over her physical virginity seems to reflect that most pernicious dichotomy, posited in the last century, between the Christ of the Faith and the historical Jesus, if indeed it is not its Mariological equivalent. Here too the truth of the Lord should be sought more in faith than in history. What matters most is the truth of the Faith and of the spirit, as opposed to the historical data on Jesus, which can be easily manipulated by the historian. In fact, concealed at the origin of this mentality of denigration towards both the historical Jesus and Mary's physical virginity lies a certain contempt for the material. The mystery is shattered by the blows of a pickax, that of mere historical criticism, and ultimately relegated to the "golden spheres" of the immaterial.

This highlights both the severe limitation and contradiction of an exegesis based on the historical-critical method when it is used as the absolute measure of evaluation. Historical criticism causes history, physical facts, and the material dimension all to be demolished. Evidently, exegetical absolutes are not sufficient for interpreting what is primarily a truth of the faith consigned by God to the Church, and which then unfolds itself in a historical context. One must therefore conflate history with Faith, Faith with Magisterium, Faith with reason, body with spirit, physical virginity with spiritual virginity.

This is the reason why we have objected strongly against Brown's exegetical style (and that of his followers), where everything, even Sacred Scripture itself, is subordinated to the historical-critical method.[115] Of course, Brown rejects the category of mere theological opinion or narrative form when addressing Mary's virginal conception,[116] since this account already existed prior to the Gospels of Matthew and Luke. However, in order to explain the fact of Mary's virginal conception in a historical-critical way, he is compelled, among other things, to engage in fanciful suppositions, since he deems his only sources, Matthew and Luke, to be insufficient to demonstrate the historicity of this mystery. Therefore, he starts with the public ministry of Jesus and then goes backwards till the very beginning of the Incarnate Word. In other words, for Brown, Jesus's virginal conception is an illumination that occurred in the minds of Matthew and Luke, the only evangelists who report Jesus's childhood, in the form of a retrospective reflection that begins at the start of the Lord's public life, and specifically at His Baptism. It is at His Baptism that the epiphany of the Holy Spirit takes place, when He descends upon Jesus, consecrating Him in His messianic mission (see Mark 1:9–11). Since Matthew's and Luke's Gospels were written after Mark's, this is the point from which the two evangelists supposedly traced their accounts back to the Lord's origins.[117]

One can understand that in so doing, the historicity and truth of Mary's virginal conception, even if not expressly denied, assumes nonetheless a merely marginal role. What would then become important are the theological reflections of the evangelists who, from the fact of Jesus's divine Sonship in His public ministry, inferred His divine Sonship in the proclamation of the angel, and thereby His virginal conception (and consequently, somehow, also His virginal birth) through Mary. One can see how in this framework everything is set up for the demolition of the truth of Mary's virginity in favor of "more important" and more compelling facts, in this case the beginning of Jesus's public ministry.

By reasoning exclusively in an historical-critical fashion, history is pitted against revealed Truth, and once again, supposition is preferred to the integrity and totality of the truth. Why not, instead, interpret the epiphany at the Jordan, with the descent of the Holy Spirit on Christ in the form of a dove, as confirmation of what had already taken place at the Annunciation? Would it not be more logical? We shall answer these questions by analyzing Brown's thinking more systematically, while adopting a more straightforward approach: interpreting the Scriptures via the method of progressive revelation, which is the way they have been handed down to us.

Mary's Virginal Conception (Matt. 1:18–25; Luke 1:30–5) and the Epiphany at the Jordan (Mark 1:9–11; Matt. 3:16–17; Luke 3:21–22)

We shall introduce this theme by posing this question: is it not more in conformity with the fullness of Scripture to place Christ's virginal conception in Mary by the Holy Spirit at the origin of His mystery, and as the prelude to God's epiphany at His Baptism in the Jordan? Or, in reverse order, is it not more realistic to consider the descent of the Holy Spirit on Jesus at His Baptism in the Jordan a public manifestation and universal inauguration of Christ's divine Sonship, originating from the Spirit's initial, hidden descent in Mary's womb, when He consecrated her as the Ever-Virgin Mother of God? Surely, this represents a powerful exegetical response to Brown.

While somehow accepting a historical revelation of Mary's virginal conception,[118] Brown explains its biblical foundation in both Matthew and Luke as the merging of two preceding traditions, through which the two evangelists were able to describe it or, rather, interpret it. In his exegesis, Brown does not start from the virginal conception of Mary as a historical reality. Nor in fact could he: by embracing entirely the historical-critical approach, he sees Scripture as a text that can only be understood by going through its historical development process. However, by addressing the text solely as if it were just words to be deciphered historically, he eclipses the most significant fact — that in fact *there is a text* in the first place. Quite often the text itself loses its significance and Scripture gets bogged down in everyday human affairs, if not in political events.

According to Brown, the two traditions preceding Matthew's and Luke's texts on Mary's virginal conception would be, firstly, the *kerygmatic* proclamation of Jesus as the Son of God generated through the Holy Spirit (as inferred from the epiphany of the Baptism in the Jordan). Matthew and Luke then applied this proclamation to the virginal conception of Christ, following a long theological reflection. Secondly, there would be a tradition concerned with the annunciation of the Davidic Messiah's birth by an angel. Supposedly, this annunciation would have been conjured up by simple folk based on Old Testament annunciations that were modified with the insertion of the figure of "a virgin" to overcome the problem of sterility.

Moreover, associating this type of annunciation to the Messiah's birth was made possible by the fact that the notion of "Son of God" in early proclamations was starting to echo that of Son of David. As Brown writes, "At the time when the concept of the generation of the Son of God had started to be applied to the conception of Jesus, the relationship between Davidic Sonship and divine Sonship had become complementary.... And if the Holy Spirit had been associated in a decisive way to the divine Sonship in Christian proclamations, a mention of the Holy Spirit in the coronation (generation) of a Davidic King and consequently of the Messiah was absolutely not out of place."[119]

With regard to this latter tradition, the difference between Matthew and Luke would be traced to the separate way in which it was developed by each evangelist: Matthew by referring to events concerning the patriarch Moses and Joseph, and Luke by taking as a model the birth of John the Baptist.[120]

Ultimately, there is a flowing of the Old Testament into the New Testament which, through the filter of the early proclamation, somehow becomes the amalgamation of the evangelical composition. In any case, in this lofty, exegetical flight of fancy, who would feel up to saying that Mary's virginal conception by the hand of the Holy Spirit is still a real or historical fact? Indeed, in Brown's view, "it must be explained why the Christology of the divine Sonship, when it is associated with the birth of Jesus, is expressed in the form of a virginal conception."

To which he answers, "I shall put forth the hypothesis that it must have required a catalyzing, historical element, and therefore I do not consider the virginal conception as a particularly adequate theological interpretation, as if the idea of divine Sonship had led automatically to the conclusion that Jesus did not have a human father."[121]

After what we have said, it is clear that, for Brown, the catalyzing historical element that contests the reality of the virginal conception, treating it as a mere theological interpretation, is precisely the apostolic proclamation of Christ's divine Sonship—in other words, the pre-evangelical tradition of the Christology of the divine Sonship via the generating power of the Holy Spirit,[122] interpreted by Matthew and Luke in the birth of Jesus to be in the form of a virginal conception brought about by the action of the Holy Spirit. Therefore, the epiphany at the Jordan would be the pivotal event providing the two evangelists, who posit Mary's virginal conception, with the hermeneutical key for the Incarnation of the Word. Hence, it would be a retrospective theological reflection, which from the beginning of the Lord's public life goes back to His actual entrance into the world, when the Word became flesh in Mary's womb. Christ was consecrated as Messiah by the Holy Spirit in the Jordan, and the Father, from Heaven, confirmed His divine Sonship (in this, the synoptics agree); in Brown's view, this is where the attribution of the virginal conception, by the action of the Holy Spirit, of Christ entering Mary's womb, comes from.

However, now the problem is this: Did the virginal conception of Christ by means of the Holy

Spirit consecrating Mary's womb ever actually take place? And, therefore, does Brown ultimately think that Christ was humanly generated? If his position is stretched further, we arrive at a duplication of Rudolph Bultmann's position.[123] If one does not accept the facts of the Gospel for what they are — if, in other words, one does not trust the history that the texts bear witness to — eventually one will inevitably get to the point of refuting the mystery itself. But then, if the mystery becomes an accretion, why continue to believe in Christ? Merely because He is a "liberator" sanctified by the Spirit at the Jordan? We know well the consequences of this false and pernicious doctrine.

We must have the courage to acknowledge — without fear of appearing less scholarly — that the most authentic catalyzing element, and the most in keeping with Scripture, is Scripture itself, including the facts that it reports and how it reports them. These facts open us up to faith in the living Christ, conceived virginally in Mary's womb by the descent of the Spirit of God and proclaimed Son of God, publicly, at the Jordan by means of the same Spirit. From the intimacy of Nazareth in which the Holy Spirit silently brought about the Incarnation of the Son of God, we arrive, by way of revelation, at the epiphanic manifestation of the Jordan, where the same Christ is acknowledged by the intervention of the Spirit as the Beloved Son of the Father.

At Nazareth, Jesus is the Son of the Father who begins to be the Son of man in Mary by means of the Spirit; He is the Son of man at the Jordan, acknowledged to be the Son of the Father by means of the Spirit. Here the true unifying factor is not so much the apostolic proclamation but rather the *sign* of Mary's virginity, which inextricably links the Son of God to the mystery of His human-divine nature. If it is possible to believe in Christ-the-man as Son of God, as occurred at the event of His Baptism, this is precisely because the Father gives to men the sign of the virginal conception of His Son in Mary's womb. Only if Mary is a virgin can the God-man be recognized in the man-God. The Virgin makes us believe that Jesus, as very man, is God. She safeguards His divinity intact without negating His humanity.

Mary's Virginal Conception (Matt. 1:18–25; Luke 1:34–35) as a Prelude to the Epiphany at the Jordan (Mark 1:9–11; Matt. 3:16–17; Luke 3:21–22)

Let us focus once more on the relationship between Mary's virginal conception and God's epiphany at the River Jordan. The details common to both mysteries are so interesting that we would readily venture to suggest that the two are in continuity and have a mutual relationship: in terms of, first, the silent entrance of the Word into this world and, second, the universal manifestation of the Son of God. Both events manifest the mystery of the Most Blessed Trinity and the two trinitarian missions outside God that proceed from the Father: the Word who becomes man and the Holy Spirit sent to sanctify, both of whom are united in generating Christ through the Spirit. At the Annunciation, the Spirit brings about the Incarnation; at the Jordan, the Spirit descending upon Christ brings about His messianic proclamation. Both at Nazareth — "the Holy which shall be born of thee shall be called the Son of God" (Luke 1:35) — and at the Jordan — "This is my beloved Son, in whom I am well pleased" (Matt. 3:17) — the Father testifies His generational relationship with the Son.

Moreover, a synoptic reading of Scripture highlights the deep connection between these two theophanies, showing them to be complementary: the Annunciation and Jesus's virginal conception, which, literally, "is of the Holy Spirit" (Matt. 1:20), mark the beginning of the era of salvation, the entrance into the world of the Son of God. The Baptism at the Jordan, on the other hand, marks the messianic manifestation of Christ to the nations and the call for everyone to become sons and daughters of the Father, in Christ, by means of the Spirit, through the announcement of the baptismal institution.

We start from Christ's virginal conception in Mary's womb and arrive at the special epiphany at the Jordan. It is not possible to go backwards from the Jordan to arrive at Nazareth. It is more logical and more in conformity with the truth of Scripture that from Nazareth we arrive at the public event of Christ's messianic anointing at the Jordan, as preparation for the final command of going all over the world to baptize all nations in the name of the Most Blessed Trinity (cf. Matt. 28:19–20). It is the Holy Spirit who guides the steps of Christ: the first steps of His entrance into the world, to prepare the way for the steps of His apostles, in all ages and to the ends of the earth.

The Annunciation and the virginal Incarnation of the Word (conception being equivalent to incarnation) mark Christ's first steps into the world, which is now the world of the Mother, her virginal womb. The descent of the Holy Spirit ensures that the horizons of Mary's world unfold to the Word and that her womb unfolds intact to the Savior by the creative action of God's Breath. The Son of God made man is already full of the Holy Spirit. It is the Son who brings down from Heaven the Father's Spirit; it is the Spirit who generates Christ's human nature, by hovering delicately over Mary, overshadowing her. At that instance, at the very beginning, by means of the Spirit, Christ is already anointed Messiah and Savior. Mary is God's earth, the world upon which the gates of the Most High are opened. In her Annunciation, she reopens those gates that had been shut following Adam's sin. The gates of the world reopen for Mary: though they were never really closed for her, since her world was always that of original creation.

The Annunciation and the virginal conception of the Word by the action of the Holy Spirit are the beginning of the new creation. The Spirit descends and forms in Mary's womb — "the firstborn amongst many brtehren" (Rom. 8:29) — so that everyone could be conformed to the image of the Son (cf. Rom. 8:29), becoming in Him "the image of the invisible God" (Col. 1:15), a "new creature" (2 Cor. 5:17). Mary is the womb of the new creation, the new earth, the virginal fragrance of God.

By accepting Jesus, she already accepts all His

brothers — that is, all disciples of Christ who are born in Him through Baptism. Mary is an untainted womb; she is the spotless creation, the spotless Church (cf. Eph. 5:27) where Christ, by means of His Spirit, is already making all things new (cf. Apoc. 21:5): in His humanity — from the Spirit and from Mary — He unveils the new things, the new world. The firstfruits of this new world, reconstituted in the Blood of the Lamb, will be the celibacy lived out by the Incarnate Word as the *ad extra* prolonging of the Son's *ad intra* act of unceasing love for the Father — a celibacy required also of His close friends, alongside the call to a life of total consecration to God through the observance of the evangelical counsels.

This new creation, which begins in Mary the Ever-Virgin, is manifested by way of public revelation at Jesus's Baptism in the River Jordan. The Son made man is immersed in the river and receives Baptism to satisfy the law fully, as Matthew tells us (3:15). His descent into the waters is like the Son's descent into the abyss of man, to restore the whole man, to wash humanity by taking upon Himself the sins of men. Christ reemerges from the waters like a new Moses leading His people out of the waters of the Red Sea, by passing through it (see Ex. 14:21–31). Like a new Joshua who leads the people through the waters of the Jordan after having walked on dry land (see Jos. 4:14–17), Christ consecrates those waters so that they may be able to heal fully in the sacrament of Baptism. Indeed, here the Fathers see the sanctification of the waters as the preparation for the Christian Baptism.

Matthew and Mark testify that as soon as Jesus emerged from the water, the heavens opened and the Spirit of God was seen descending on Jesus in the form of a dove. The Spirit then literally hovers over the waters. That same Spirit that hovered over the waters of creation (see Gen. 1:1–2), now descending upon Christ the firstborn of the new creation, reveals that Jesus is the new creation, publicly and formally consecrated as Messiah "with the Holy Ghost, and with power" (Acts 10:38). While already full of the Holy Spirit since His conception, now the age of the new beginning is preeminently the age of the Spirit according to the prophets (cf. Is. 61:1), and therefore he who baptizes with the Spirit must himself experience the formal anointing of the Spirit. This present anointing is connected to the formal initiation of His ministry, which is itself based on the twofold aspect of the royal crowning of the Messiah (cf. Ps. 2) and of the commission of YHWH's Servant (cf. Is. 42:1).[124] This parallel between creation and the new creation is revealed publicly at the Jordan as the continuation and resonance of the epiphany at Nazareth and is rendered possible also by the fact that, already in the Old Testament, the liberation of Israel from slavery and from the solitude of dispersion was considered an event of a new creation (see Deut. 32:5–12), carried out under the shadow of God's cloud or of the pillar of fire (see Ex. 12:21–22 in light of John 1:1–2).

Finally — and we see this also in Luke 3:22 along with the other two Synoptics — the Father's voice testifies that Jesus is His Beloved Son in whom He is well-pleased. Through the sign of the Holy Spirit visibly descending upon Him — unlike His invisible descent upon Mary at the Annunciation — Jesus testifies that in His human nature as servant, He who became man like us is God, is the Son of God. The intimacy of Nazareth is the prelude to Christ's mystery, God made flesh by the work of the Holy Spirit. We cannot then but concur with Benedict XVI when he says, "Is it not more logical, also from the historical point of view, that greatness is located at the outset and that the figure of Jesus has practically overturned all the available categories and could thus be understood only by starting from the mystery of God?"[125]

Matthew and Luke, Witnesses
of Jesus's Virginal Conception

Let us start again from a primary and fundamental truth: Scripture does not deceive us, and we can trust it by accepting what it tells us. The books of the Bible that Tradition has consigned to us are faithful to what the authors wanted to tell us. If I doubt the Scriptures and their historical veracity, I surely doubt God Himself. God breaks into and through our history, and through history we can go back to the God who speaks, but on one condition: that history is true (that the facts correspond to reality), and that the truth is historical. But for this to be possible, it is necessary for God to speak, and not man.

Therefore, if I admit that God speaks to me, if I accept His truth, I trust Scripture as His historical word: His word which, moreover, proclaims a message of salvation to me, a message that transcends its own past to reach me in my time here and now. God speaks to me today through a spoken Word that does not change. Hence, to understand what God is saying to me today through a Word He has already spoken, I must trust what He said to me and the way He said it so that His Word can reach me now. It is no less scientific to trust the Gospels by believing what they tell us than to start from a basic agnosticism that often leads us to ignore the very same God who is speaking. Quite the opposite.

It is He who has spoken in various ways, and in recent times, He has spoken through His Son (see Heb. 1:1–12). Frequently, by dissecting the Scriptures, you end up setting yourself up against them. The divergences between different authors in reporting the same event are not always a sign of inferior historicity and editorial accretions; instead, they are generally a sign of a human account of events that, in their substance, have occurred exactly in the way they were recounted. And in our context, this is particularly true of the accounts of Jesus's childhood.

In the eyes of right reason, a mere theological opinion, or something comparable, that relativizes the virginal conception of the Lord is less scientific than the historical truth of Jesus's birth from Mary by the action of the Holy Spirit, since such opinion is artificial and contrived. Mystery is a key ingredient in the accounts of the synoptic Gospels of Matthew and Luke, which present God's supernatural action. Eliminating or diluting this mystery renders the text less reliable because it is less scientific. Science is always at the service of God, of mystery and of Holy Scripture, and never the other way round.

In any case, when comparing the first two chapters of Matthew with the first two of Luke, one thing stands out for the reader: despite not having a single episode in common, the accounts are not heterogeneous; on the contrary, they coincide on all the fundamental historical details—beginning with the characters involved: Jesus, Mary, Joseph, Herod; the places: Nazareth, Bethlehem, with reference to Jerusalem; and the dating: we are at the time of Herod the Great, shortly before his death (cf. Matt. 2:1–22; Luke 1:5). René Laurentin writes, "In history the concordantia discordantium (convergence of differences) is the best test for the critical authentication of the testimonies."[126]

Notably, Matthew's Gospel presents some stylistic peculiarities—given the Jewish context of its development and the author's affiliation with Judaic tradition—that underscore an interesting fact: Matthew is bound by the facts and not simply, as some argue, by prophesies, so as to make the New Testament appear as the fulfillment of the Old. One need only consider that in his genealogy of Christ he also includes four women: Tamar, Ruth, Bathsheba—not expressly named but indicated as "the wife of Uriah"—and Rahab (see Matt. 1:1–17), whereas by contrast, Eve's daughters were never included in genealogies.[127] These four women prepared the solemn entrance of the Woman, Mary, "of whom was born Jesus, who is called Christ" (Matt. 1:16).

While all other women generated offspring by union with a man, only Mary, the Woman, did not do so; this is even more surprising, not just for the naming of another woman, but also for the absence of any mention of the generating man, as there was none. Consequently, Laurentin urges, "What counts for our discourse is that Matthew 1–2 did not invent the childhood at Nazareth starting from a biblical text, as a small number of exegetes have argued, but, rather, he laboriously adapted the biblical texts to account for the childhood at Nazareth."[128]

There is no irrational theological fervor (not to say delirium!) from the author as he constructs the accounts of the childhood of the Lord; on the contrary, he inserts the accounts as they are, even when they strongly conflict with the prevailing popular understanding. Similarly, the insertion of the way Jesus died hanging from a cross was certainly not done to pay homage to the Lord, and neither was it an uplifting pledge for the long-term success of his proclamation!

Let us return once more to Matthew's genealogy and then back to Luke's genealogy. Luke's genealogy begins with Jesus, who was believed to be Joseph's son even if He was not (largely in agreement with Matthew; see Luke 3:23), and traces His ancestry all the way back to the first man, Adam. One of the first novelties that characterizes the manifestation of Jesus, the "God with us" (Matt. 1:23), through the abrupt break in the genealogical line is that Joseph—who Matthew never indicates as the father of Jesus—is excluded from the physical paternity of Jesus. This is even more remarkable than what we said earlier, given that in the Jewish culture the concept of "parents" (in the etymological sense of both being "generators") did not exist: only the father was considered to be the parent generating the son, while the mother was the one giving birth to him (cf. Is. 45:10). In generating his son, the father not only bestowed life to him but by giving him his name, he bestowed on him also his religious and moral heritage. The tradition of Israel is perpetuated from father to son, and the firstborn male would carry the father's name (see Num. 27:4). By contrast, Jesus is generated solely by a woman, according to the flesh. Already here one can detect in both Evangelists at least the foreshadowing of a divine and miraculous intervention, something, after all, not unusual in the history of Israel.

The fact that Joseph was not a generator, a reality that was disconcerting relative to customary practice, is extremely valuable information in support of the historical authenticity of Matthew and Luke's texts on the childhood of Jesus. As it happens, in the end, this genealogical interruption did not constitute a propitious discovery but rather a failure of the apologetic discourse in favor of the real existence of Jesus. In fact, this information denied the Davidic-Messianic ancestry of Christ (according to the Joseph's lineage).[129] Both Evangelists, however, compensate for this sudden interruption by emphasizing the historical fact that Jesus was born in Bethlehem, David's birthplace. This event confirmed Micah's messianic prophecy (5:1–5), according to which the Messiah was to be born in Bethlehem.[130] The Messiah was God Himself who was to come. He "will claim" to be God since He was a Messiah different from human expectations, but in full accordance with the Scriptures.

MARY'S VIRGINAL BIRTH: "AND THEREFORE ALSO THE HOLY WHICH SHALL BE BORN OF THEE SHALL BE CALLED THE SON OF GOD" (LUKE 1:35)

We shall now focus on the mystery of Mary's virginal birth. It is more necessary than ever to repeat tirelessly that Mary's virginity is not a purely spiritual or moral fact, as is posited today, but it is *principally* and *directly* a physical fact: it concerns her inviolate body before, during, and after the birth. Relegating Mary's virginity to the domain of the heart excludes one from the faith of the Church. Either her virginity is, first and foremost, something physical or it is not virginity in *strictu sensu*. Certainly, we can talk of a virginity of the heart, but this is an analogical way of speaking that presupposes the physical-corporeal element; otherwise, the very essence of virginity cannot be realized.

Unfortunately, today, at a time when the body's dignity and the importance of virginity and chastity for the Kingdom of Heaven is questioned, one is pummeled by the many storms striking the Church's two-thousand-year-old Tradition. And few people are raising their voices. Few are even aware that the faith of the Church is being eroded from the inside to the point of becoming disrupted and secularized. Our Lady is Ever-Virgin. She is a virgin even at the most sublime and serene moment of her giving birth. Holy Scripture testifies to this, regardless of what certain exegetes more aligned to the world than to the Word of God might have to say.[131]

A magnificent text that we have read many times, though perhaps rather hastily, and that truly sheds light on the mystery of Mary's virginal birth is the one in Luke 1:35b. Most of the translations read thus: "He who shall be born shall therefore be holy and called the Son of God." If one carefully examines the original Greek, one notices a peculiarity of the phrase in question: "Kaì tò gennómenon àgion klethésetai uiòs Theû" (What will be generated [will be born] holy, shall be called the Son of God). "Holy" becomes the predicate of "will be born," which is the equivalent of an adverb (holily). This translation brought to light by St. Zedda, is taken up with noteworthy emphasis by Ignace de la Potterie.

From this, it becomes clear that the angel's Annunciation to Mary refers also to the *manner* of the Lord's birth. Jesus will be born of Mary in a holy way, which is to say in a virginal manner. Therefore, it can be properly translated as "He Who will be born holy will be called the Son of God." Jesus is the virginal fruit of Mary's womb. Here the adverbial predicate "holy," which concurs with the present passive participle "will be born," is to be understood according to its divine-biblical character. God is the thrice holy (cf. Is. 6:3), which means that He is separated from man in an inaccessible realm. The Mother who generates virginally (that is, in a holy manner) does so in a way that is inaccessible to men — a way that is not human but divine, untainted, and pure (of a purity that befits divine holiness). Moreover, Jesus's virginal birth from Mary will be the authentic *sign* that the One being born is the Son of God. The One that will be born in a holy manner will be the Son of God. God, who is the All Holy, cannot but be born in a holy manner through Mary the All Holy. Throughout the ages, this will be the *visible sign* that He is the Son of God, fully divine like the Father.

Ignace de la Potterie writes, "The angel's message to Mary contains then not only the annunciation of the virginal conception, but also that of Jesus's virginal birth."[132]

St. Cyril of Jerusalem affirms this thesis in his commentary on Luke: "His birth was pure and untainted, since wherever the breath of the Holy Spirit blows every stain is removed. The physical birth of the Only-Begotten Son was therefore untainted."[133]

De la Potterie continues:

If we carefully read Luke's verse 1:35, we can then distinguish three elements:

• The virginal conception: "The Holy Spirit shall come upon thee." Mary will conceive a Son by the power of the Holy Spirit and not by man's intervention;

• The virginal birth: "And therefore also the Holy which shall be born of thee. . . . " Nine months after the virginal conception a "holy" birth will take place (that is, a ritually pure, untainted birth);

- The future of the child that will be born: "He shall be called the Son of God."

In virtue of the virginal conception, and, above all, of the virginal birth which is its sign ("therefore also"), this child, in the course of his public life, and afterwards, shall be called "the Son of God.". . . The difference between the conception and the birth consists principally in this: the virginal conception took place secretly, in Mary's womb. The birth, and, above all, the circumstances of this birth (no body lesions for the mother and thus no loss of blood: "Non ex sanguinibus" John will declare later), are the exterior sign. The two moments taken together would be considered subsequently as a "sign" of Jesus's divine Sonship. . . .

Based on a precise exegesis of Luke 1:35, we may say then that the virginal birth is an exterior "sign" necessary for men to accept Jesus's divine Sonship. He is the Son of God, given that God Himself is His Father, not Joseph: the virginal birth is the sign of this.[134]

Mary's Virginal Birth: "But of God [He] was born" (John 1:13)

In this section, let us search for a new scriptural testimony concerning Mary's virginity, particularly her virginity during the birth, which can verify the biblical foundation of this revealed truth taught by councils and the papal Magisterium.

A very important text where we can easily detect Mary's *virginitas in partu* is St. John's Prologue; here is where we routinely read that Jesus Himself gave the power to become sons of God to those who have received the Word that was coming into the world—in other words, to "those who were born, not of blood, nor of the will of the flesh, nor of the will of man, but of God" (John 1:13). We shall now address in detail the words, "those who were born."

The now deceased scholar de la Potterie, one of the foremost experts on John's Gospel, points out that if the Prologue is analyzed in its entirety, the words "those who were born" (referring to the sons of God, those who accepted Jesus) could well be translated into the singular version "he who was born," in reference to Jesus Himself and to His temporal generation.[135]

This interpretation—which is also featured in multiple testimonies within the Latin translations of the fifth century, including Irenaeus, Origen, Tertullian, Jerome, and Augustine—is favored by the French scholar for several illuminating reasons.[136] Admittedly, when reading the Prologue verses preceding and following the one under scrutiny (verse 13), it does truly seem that a plural sense of the words falls outside the intention of the author, who refers (in the singular) to Christ in both verse 11 ("He came unto his own") and verse 14 ("And the Word was made flesh"). Accordingly, if one attempts to decipher the full meaning of verse 13, the singular sense can be accommodated without forcing the text. In this way, the subject of the sentence is Jesus, "He who" "was born, not of blood, nor of the will of the flesh, nor of the will of man, but of God." Here also the Greek verb agrees with the singular version as it is rendered in the third person singular (*egennethe*), "was born," instead of the third person plural (*egennéthesan*). It is Christ who was generated. Thus, the ground is prepared for the solemn opening of the next verse, which in a certain sense is the heart of John's Gospel: "And the Word was made flesh, and dwelt among us" (John 1:14).

Once again, it is important to correctly grasp the significance of Christ's generation. We know that Christ, being the Word of the Father, is generated from all eternity. The Word proceeds from the Father and is always with the Father (as stated in verse 1 of the Prologue). Moreover, the Word who comes to dwell among His people is the *Logos* made flesh, as described by St. John in verse 14. Hence, "generation," in the verse under examination, and in light of those verses that immediately precede and follow it, can only be the temporal generation of the Incarnate Word. Christ was generated in time *by God* through Mary. He is made flesh without the help of man and solely by the power of God, by the power of the Holy Spirit (cf. Luke 1:34) who overshadows Mary, renders her virginally fecund, and enables her to give birth virginally. Here we glimpse both the virginal conception of the Word in Mary's womb as well as her virginal birth. God (the Father) is the origin of both the eternal and human generation of the Word. Christ has only one Father, from whom He proceeds as the *Logos*, and from whom He comes in His human generation in the Mother's womb by the power of the Holy Spirit.

What then greatly emphasizes Mary's virginal birth is the fact that Jesus is generated "not of bloods," and also in the absence of "the will of the flesh" and "the will of man." In other words, it is a virginal conception without any human involvement. Of note is the distinction of that "not of bloods" in the original Greek, compared to the "not of blood" in the Italian translation. The absence of "bloods" has been interpreted by some exclusively as Mary's virginal conception, with no involvement from any man. In reality, the "bloods," as emphasized by de la Potterie and confirmed by ancient Greek literature, alludes to the virginal birth by the Mother of God — namely, to the absence of the loss of blood at the birth. Thereby, we are looking at a pure, holy, virginal birth. In Mary's parturition, no physical-structural lesions occurred and thus no labor pains, even though it was clearly a real birth. Christ passes through His Mother's members leaving them intact. Mary, for her part, is still Jesus's real Mother because she truly gave birth to Him, although in a manner that befitted the human-divine mystery of that Son. Mary's virginal birth is the *sign* that He who passes is the Son of the Father and not a mere man (see Ez. 44:2, a text referred to by the Church Fathers in relation to the virginal birth); He "who is not of bloods but of God was born."

Moreover, Mary's birth is a virginal birth, which undoes the condemnation directed at the woman in Genesis 3:16: "in sorrow shalt thou bring forth children." As Serra explains, "With the entry of the Redeeming Messiah into the world (as Judaism had already intuitively understood) a new order arises. We return to the original harmony of things."[137]

A Parallel between Luke 1:34–35 and John 1:13–14

We shall open this new reflection on Mary's virginity by starting with a logical assertion: if Mary is not *always* a virgin, we have reduced Jesus to a mere man, nothing more. This does not seem to be a daring conclusion for the world we live in, which *would like* Jesus to be a mere man. A God-man is somewhat irksome, even tedious; He would claim to tell us how man should live in order to reach God and how God speaks to man. Much better to have a man-god; in other words, a man who makes himself into a god. Accordingly, how many relegate the Mother of God to the condition of a mere woman, perhaps even a special woman, when they are not demeaning her as "an everyday working woman!" Nothing more than that. While these days it is ever so easy to come across a minimalist, low profile "ferial Mariology," it is ever more difficult to find a Christian thoroughly professing the Faith of the Church in its entirety.

Yet, if Mary did not conceive and give birth to that Son in a holy way, in a way actually worthy of the Son *of the Most High* (cf. Luke 1:32, a genitive prepositional phrase that distinguishes YHWH from men, as God who is above and beyond everything and everyone), we will have subverted the supernatural principle of the Faith. The Faith would then become nothing more than the other face of the secularized world, another version of a culture that no longer has any room for God.

In truth, we believe in a God-Man who, as we said, gives us the Virgin-Mother as a *sign* of His transcendence (a sign being the unity of a tangible element and the intelligible one it points to). As the Virgin Mother, she is the assurance of the true Faith. She is the bastion of Catholicism, and this is why we must strenuously oppose any attempt to secularize her.

Previously, I sought to shed light on the mystery of Mary's virginity by recalling an exegetical key that is most enlightening and most in keeping with the *analogia fidei* of the Scriptures, and with the harmonious symbiosis that exists between Old and New Testaments, and between each book and the Bible as a whole. I believe, alongside a number of illustrious scholars, that the canonical (analogical) method of reading the Holy Scriptures explains more effectively the content of two fundamental texts: Luke 1:35 and John 1:13, especially the way they express the truth of Mary's virginal conception (cf. John 1:13) and particularly her virginal birth as a continuation of the original mystery of her conception in both texts. As de la Potterie writes, "The virginal birth and the virginal conception form together a single process; they are the beginning and the end of that period (of gestation); but the birth, even more than the conception, is a sign of God's intervention in the incarnation of the Word: the virginal birth was a sign of the virginal conception, a sign of the fact that the Word Incarnate was 'generated by God.' Therefore, the first Christians, in contemplating the Word Incarnate in the light of His human generation, understood that He was 'the Only-Begotten Son coming from the Father.'"[138]

For this reason, there can be no naturalistic motives that may be cobbled together to denigrate, or reduce to the merely spiritual level, the truth of Mary's virginity, which, as we can see, acts as the hinge between God the Most High and the truth of man. Mary's virginity is God's gate into the world, the passage of God. God *passes* only through purity and integrity, which is why only "the pure of heart will see God" (Matt. 5:8).

God is absolute purity. St. Mary Magdalene of Pazzi would say that "purity is God's being and the God's being is purity." Now, this Being-Purity begins to be that which He was not beforehand, without ceasing to be what He has always been, and by renewing what He was: purity. Mary is, in a manner of speaking, God's purity in time. She is the sacred vessel that welcomes God-Purity and brings Him to light in precisely what God Himself is, purity. To deny this mystery is to deny God; it is to say that God is like us, perhaps lower than us, but in any case not greater than us. Denying this is a cover for the devious leitmotif of wanting to divinize oneself without being what God is, and thus to become a god, making oneself into a god, but in so doing setting oneself against Him.

Comparing texts by Luke and John shows close-up the aforementioned *analogia fidei*, highlighting even more clearly the virginal-mystery we are addressing. Below is a synoptic overview of Luke 1:34–35 (the annunciation of the virginity) and of John 1:13–14 (its fulfillment):

Synopsis	Luke 1:34–35	John 1:13–14
Generation	I know not man The power of the Most High Shall overshadow thee	Nor of the will of man, but of God (Jesus was generated)
Birth	The Holy which shall be born of thee	Who (Jesus) is born, not of blood
Recognition	Shall be called the Son of God	And we saw His glory, the glory of the Only Begotten of the Father

In this way, as de la Potterie points out,[139] we can see that Luke and John are united in the same will to communicate Mary's virginal conception and virginal birth, both linked to the mystery of the Incarnation of the Son of God in the context of the economy of Revelation. Luke expresses this by way of the Annunciation (he is the only one to report the angel's Annunciation to our Lady, in the manner of a grand master painting), and John by way of its fulfillment: his entire Gospel aims to show that God's Revelation has been fulfilled in Jesus, who was generated by God, and that He, as His Son, reveals the Father so that those who believe in Him have life eternal (see John 1:13, 18; 20:31, the beginning and the end of the fourth Gospel).

The Ever-Virgin Mary is the "invincible fortress" of the revelation of the Son of God. If the Mother is cherished, the Son is cherished, and the Son's true identity is cherished only if she is cherished in truth. Without Mary's virginity, there is no *recognition* of Jesus; His glory does not shine.

MARY'S VIRGINITY AFTER THE BIRTH:
"I KNOW NOT MAN" (LUKE 1:34)

Having addressed the mystery of our Lady's virginity *before* and *during* the birth, particularly *during* the birth — which, as we have seen, has become a "problem" for some thinkers — we now turn our attention to Mary's virginity *after* the birth. Namely, something that is already in some way understandable as a necessary consequence: what would be the sense of an integral virginity before and during the birth of Jesus if it was to be lost afterwards? Was it simply to acknowledge the Son of God come in the flesh, but from a simple mother like all the others?

We exclude as pure conjecture the possibility that Jesus had any blood siblings. In fact, in both the Hebrew and Aramaic languages, the word "brother" was applied not only to "children of the same mother" but also more broadly to also encompass cousins, nephews, brothers-in-law, relatives, and even friends — in other words, all those who in some way were part of the extended family nucleus. James and Joses (in Mark), or Joseph (in Matthew), identified as the brothers of Jesus in Mark 6:3 and in Matthew 13:55, most probably were the sons of a woman called Maria, who was certainly not the Mother of Jesus. She was the same Mary who was called "the mother of Joses" in Mark 15:47 and "of James and Salome" in Mark 16:1. Even in Luke, "Mary [the mother] of James" is mentioned (24:10). It should be noted yet again that the brothers and sisters of Jesus are never identified as children of Mary. Only Jesus is "the Son of Mary," and Mary is identified solely as the "mother of Jesus." Furthermore, if Mary had had other children, she would not have left them to be with her Son's disciples and then ultimately with John.[140]

The idea of Jesus having siblings certainly did not come only from neo-Arians, such as the Jehovah Witnesses. It began circulating in the fourth century with the heretic Helvetius (who thought that, in doing so, the superiority of marriage over virginity could be proved, a heresy subsequently silenced by St. Jerome) and with Bonosus, bishop of Sardica, who was, however, abandoned as a heretic following the intervention of St. Ambrose.

Let us return to our starting point. Mary losing her virginity after having given birth to Jesus would be simply incomprehensible and, at best, unworthy of God Himself, who, having announced to Mary His desire for the virginal Incarnation of His Son, would have subsequently given in to His Mother's "personal choices." No, either Mary is the Ever-Virgin or she has never been a virgin, meaning she would simply not be Mary: "The name of the Virgin was Mary" (Luke 1:27).

Admittedly, the Scriptures do not contain a direct and formal text on Mary's virginity after the birth. However, this does not alter the fact that we ought to pay attention to the Scriptures in their entirety and, above all, read them with the Faith of the Church to which they were given. In her professions of Faith and magisterial declarations since the early Apostolic Fathers, the Church has always recognized Mary as the perpetual Virgin, linking her integral virginity to the truth of the Incarnation of Christ. Suffice it to mention the Nicene Creed (325–381), which we profess every Sunday at Holy Mass, "Et incarnatus est ex Maria Virgine." Therefore, the Scriptures do not disappoint in this regard, as indeed they never do. Obviously, this is not about inventing superfluous things or making pious rather than scientific accommodations, but about paying attention to the Scriptures with the *auditus fidei* matured over the Christian millennia.

Luke's text reporting the angel's annunciation to Mary offers us a magnificent clue in understanding the faith of the Church in the Ever-Virgin: at the Annunciation of the Incarnation of the Word in her womb, Mary does not renounce her maternity, but she does pose an important qualification: "How shall this be done, because I know not man?" (Luke 1:34). That is to say: "How can what you tell me happen if, in the secret of my heart, I have promised God that I would preserve my virginity intact?"[141] She wants to obey God and at the same time glorify Him with a total self-offering by simply excluding the normal life experience as a wife, albeit the wife of a holy man. In any case, Mary knows that He who created everything with His Word can even create Himself in her womb without man's intervention. Is this a thesis that goes too far beyond the text? It does not seem so, since, if she does not have a sense of the greatness of Almighty God, the question she asks the angel would have been at the very least irreverent, as

if engaging in rhetorical musings that already anticipate a rejection of God's will. This is impossible, as
can be clearly inferred when we are confronted with
the muteness of Zachariah, which resulted from his
disbelief in God's creative power (see Luke 1:18–20).

Mary speaking with the angel of God wanted to
remain a virgin perpetually. Why would she have
manifested such a lofty intention at that moment if it
had been linked only to the birth of the Son of God,
of whom she had not even heard before then? Mary
is troubled because she had never thought of herself
as the Mother of the Messiah: this is the guarantee of
the perpetuity of her intention. "I know not man";
therefore, it only makes sense if understood as "I do
not want to know man, as long as I shall live." And
the Tradition of the Church is unanimous in seeing
this truth, a reality that imposes itself unequivocally,
albeit indirectly, on the reader.

Matthew 1:25 might cause some doubt, but this
doubt vanishes when the verse is contextualized. Here
the Evangelist, when speaking of the manner of the
Lord's birth, concludes the passage by mentioning
Joseph, who did not know his bride "until [donec]
she brought forth her firstborn son." It would seem
that "not knowing Mary," which means not having
conjugal relations with her, is limited until the birth
of Jesus, and after that, conjugal relations were pursued. In reality, the temporal conjunction "until,"
which defines the duration of a period limited by
a deadline or target, in biblical language indicates
primarily the temporary aspect, which in our case

is the time up to the birth of the firstborn, without excluding the continuation of Mary's virginity and thus the chastity of both spouses.

We find the same logic with John the Baptist, who it is said remained "in the deserts until the day of his manifestation to Israel" (Luke 1:80), without excluding his stay in those regions afterwards. Indeed, what is evident in the phrase is the fact that until the day of his prophetic manifestation, John stayed in the desert, but this does not thereby imply that he did not remain in the desert after his manifestation. On the contrary, even in his actions as the precursor of the Messiah the desert was where he lived and conducted his mission (see Luke 7:24–27; Matt. 3:1).

The "until" (Matt. 1:25) of our passage is linked, in its syntactic construction, to "Now the generation of Christ was in this wise [way]" (Matt. 1:18) and by no means intends to extend to the subsequent life of the holy couple, Mary and Joseph. It is therefore to be read simply in the context of the miraculous birth of the Lord. As evidence of this, the second chapter begins with the visit of the Magi.

Finally, we can also include yet another biblical witness to Mary's virginity after the birth, an Old Testament text that, while not a direct or formal witness, is neither just simply accommodating. The text is from Ezekiel (44:2). In it the prophet himself narrates how he was carried into the land of Israel and placed in front of the temple by the hand of the Lord (see Ez. 40:1–5). Led to the external door of the sanctuary facing East, it was closed (see Ez. 44:1) and a mysterious man — an angel of the Lord — whose aspect was like that of bronze, said to him: "This gate shall be shut, it shall not be opened, and no man shall pass through it: because the Lord the God of Israel hath entered in by it, and it shall be shut" (Ez. 44:2). The text alludes to the future temple in a religiously and politically restructured Palestine after the plight of the exile.

Without too much of a stretch, the Fathers (especially St. Ambrose and St. Augustine), considering the entire truth of Revelation centered on Christ, applied this text to the Virgin Mary. In particular, St. Ambrose (as well as St. Jerome, as we have seen previously) recognize in Mary "the gate that was shut and was not opened."[142] Mary, for St. Ambrose, is the *"porta clausa,"* as all the great Latin Church Fathers would chant subsequently.[143] The patristic reference is precisely regarding her virginity during the birth. But if Mary is a "closed gate" during the birth, she will be even more so afterwards. Mary is the inviolable gate of God into the world. This gate "shall be shut." *Inviolata, integra, et casta es Maria,* as the liturgy sings.

MARY "VIRGO PERPETUA"

For the Church Fathers of the fourth and fifth centuries, faith in Mary's virginity was already an established fact: Christ had been born virginally from the Ever-Virgin Mary. After the precious witnesses of St. Ignatius of Antioch (†ca. 110), St. Justin (†ca. 165), and St. Irenaeus (†ca. 200), we encounter an important text by the bishop of Salamis, St. Epiphanius (†403), whereby the adjective "ever-virgin" becomes part of the Creed (the Symbol of the Faith) as a technical formula to specify a truth of the Faith: Christ comes from "Mary, Ever-Virgin," which is stated in the Council of Constantinople II in the year 553. The article of Faith says this: "He became incarnate in Mary, the holy and glorious Ever-Virgin, Mother of God."[144]

St. Epiphanius writes, "Has anyone in any generation ever dared to say the name of Mary and not added immediately 'the Virgin,' if questioned?"[145]

For the Fathers, this is an indisputable fact. Mary is "the Virgin" (in St. Justin's writings, for example, this title appears fourteen times), and it is virginity that spans every dimension of her life. We are dealing here with a nominal adjective, *"the"* Virgin, which echoes Isaiah's prophecy (7:14) and which acknowledges a historical continuity without admitting any separation in Mary's life between *before* and *after* the birth of her Son, the Messiah. From the very beginning of the Church, "the Virgin" appeared as a designation for our Lady. Virgin is Mary's name, and Mary is the Virgin. St. Augustine, in recalling his trusted master St. Ambrose, would define the Mother of God as "perpetual virgin,"[146] thus summarizing Mary's mystery with respect to the Incarnate Word.

As we have said, there are no explicit biblical texts on the mystery of the uninterrupted virginity of the Mother of God. However, the *reality* of Mary, the Virgin—"the virgin was called Mary" (Luke 1:27), such that the nominal adjective could be used instead of the name — impressed itself so strongly upon the faith of the Church that ecclesial tradition unanimously believed and vigorously defended the truth of Mary's perpetual virginity. It is perpetual in the sense of the *semper virginitas* discussed by St. Epiphanius, which encompasses the beginning and the entire course of Mary's life, right to the end. Christ, the One who fills all things (cf. Eph. 4:10), had filled Mary's womb with grace and charity. He had consecrated it and sealed it off, for His being alone, thus becoming the Savior of humanity in Mary.

Christ is "the Alpha and the Omega, the Beginning and the End" (Apoc. 21:6), and Mary is the sacred vessel of this plenitude. There is no room in her for anything else but the love of her Son. He fills Mary with Himself, and the *I* of Mary is fully "Christified." Hence, when she ponders in her heart over her Son (see Luke 2:19), it takes on a new light. Mary lives continually in and through the memory of the Son; the Son is engrafted in her, and she lives for and through the Son. She meditates on Him, adores Him, and loves Him. Christ is everything in Mary's womb and in her mind. In and through the Son, whom she treasures, she will know and love her other children.

The Son who Mary had conceived in her womb and whom she had miraculously yet truly given birth to, was the Son of God and at the same time "her firstborn son" (Luke 2:7). Of course, this does not compromise the absence of subsequent children, since "firstborn," in the Jewish sense of this word, was not simply the first child but principally the child who personally enjoyed particular rights, such as his father's heritage. Moreover, the Son, being the Word, is the firstborn of the Father, who brought Him into the world (see Heb. 1:6).

It is precisely thanks to Mary's virginal flesh that Jesus would be "the firstborn of many brothers" (Rom. 8:29), although He had no siblings according to the flesh. Jesus would be the *protòtokon* of the new creation, *from* the Father *in* the Holy Spirit *for* Mary and only *for* Mary. For Mary to have had more natural children — such are the fantasies of the clueless and the prejudiced — would not only have been unfitting and unworthy for the Virgin and ultimately for God but also be completely detached from Scripture. This is because it would have compromised the ability to be the firstborn of Christ when it comes to His members, as well as Christ being the firstborn of the Father.[147]

Mary's firstborn is truly "the firstborn from the dead" (Col. 1:18), the "first begotten of the dead, and the prince of the kings of the earth" (Apoc. 1:5). Christ's primogeniture from Mary, reflecting in time His eternal primogeniture from the Father, is the sign of God's redeeming alliance with His people, definitively ratified through Christ. Christ, the firstborn of the Father and the firstborn of Mary, by being generated according to the flesh, brings to fulfillment the definitive universalization of God's Kingdom. It is a kingdom that no longer has any barriers of language, peoples, and nations (see Apoc. 5:9–10), but where all are called to establish the one and only people of

God, journeying towards the heavenly homeland. In Christ the firstborn, every man is called to salvation, every man *can* see God by gazing at the face of His Son (see John 12:45; 14:9).

Mary's perpetual virginity — especially her virginity after the birth — becomes, then, God's definitive seal on the new Sonship of every man in Christ — from the fullness of Christ in Mary to the fullness of Christ in us, through the perennial virginity of the Mother. It is the assurance of Christ's presence in us, of the possibility of God being in us and with us. Truly, without a doubt, in the Incarnate Word, we have "grace for grace" (John 1:16), since Mary has been entirely filled with His grace, including that of her perpetual virginity.

Mary's virginity represents the prospect of welcoming every man into the Church, as a son in the Son, begotten not according to the flesh but in the Spirit (cf. John 3:6). Mary *Virgo perpetua* is the definitive, spousal *yes* of God to man, until the end of time, to usher us into the realm of God's eternity. Mary's virginal perpetuity becomes the perpetuity of our being with God. Mary *Ever-Virgin* will be the sweet melody resounding throughout God's infinite heavens as the echo of being with Him *forever*.

In his writings, St. Irenaeus († ca. 200) emphasizes the excellence and necessity of Mary's pure womb: "The Son of God becomes the son of man, who, since He is the pure one, opened purely that pure womb which generates men unto God and which He Himself has rendered pure."[148]

CHAPTER 4

Mary's Virginity as the Hermeneutical Key of the "Kingdom of God" in Christ

"Cum ergo ad intelligendum sacramentum nativitatis Christi, qua de matre virgine est ortus, accedimus, abigatur procul terrenarum *caligo rationum*"[149]

BY WAY OF COMPLETION, we now wish to reflect on how the truth of Mary's virginity can be the hermeneutical key for a proper understanding of the Kingdom of God announced by Jesus in His messianic proclamation. Mary preserves the spiritual meaning and supernatural content of God's Kingdom. Mary's truth brings forth in a fitting way the truth of Christ and of the Gospel.

We shall focus on Mary's *theological virginity*,[150] which we believe plays a fundamental role in the proper understanding of the announcement, historical development, and eschatological fulfillment of God's Kingdom. By safeguarding the full truth of Mary's virginity, we also safeguard the full truth of Christ's announcement.

Mary's virginity is like a divine *seal* placed on the affairs of God in this world. It is akin to an assurance that it is God who operates in history and not man. It is easy to deviate from the right understanding of the "Kingdom of God" (Mark 4:11). At times it is seen as an earthly empire; at other times merely as an intimate spiritual occurrence; and yet at other times as a total rupture from what Christ wanted, the Kingdom having degenerated with the birth of the Church. All these perspectives are wrong since they fail to recognize God's righteous action. Instead, one should be asking: What could God have done in the world? What did He really want to build?

Moreover, to properly understand God's action in Christ, we must go back to an archetypal representation that can somehow model His entire work, while also conferring to it a clear, divine imprint. In our view, this archetypal representation of God's operation can be discerned in the mystery of Mary Ever-Virgin, a mystery that is both human and divine, a work/sign of God asking for man's consent and for his response of faith. In Mary's virginity, we have, as in a primordial foreshadowing, that golden and mysterious interplay between God's gift, His sublime and omnipotent primacy, and the liberty of man, intended as man's response to the gift that fulfills the mystery of human liberty.

I emphasize in this work Mary's virginity over her Immaculate Conception because it more clearly emphasizes the divine-human interplay as the "visible seal" of the *Deus-homo*. I am referring to Mary's virginity as the sign given by God to enable the acknowledgment of the Creator and of the supernatural nature of His message. In this sense, Mary's perpetual virginity acquires immense theological importance for God's operation in history; it is also foundational because through it, other signs can also be perceived and understood. For example, only by positing Mary's perpetual virginity can the magnitude and significance of the manifestation of Christ's Resurrection in His real body be fully grasped.

In fact, "the virginal conception is the first foreshadowing of the Resurrection."[151] Mary's physical virginity — namely, her bodily integrity — already points to the mystery of Christ's Resurrection in His real body, and it sheds a light on it, not as a mere metahistorical mystery, but as the eschatological fulfillment of the flesh in the plenitude of the gift of bodily glorification, thereby heralding the resurrection of the body.[152] Mary's virginity is *in primis* the gift of man's bodily glorification so that the *eschaton* of the Kingdom, which is definitively fulfilled in Christ, may *already* be proclaimed. Mary proclaims Christ and leads us fully to Him.

Furthermore, Mary is always found at the *beginning*. "Mary's place is that of the beginning."[153] Her *Fiat* resonates at the announcement of the Incarnation of the Son of God, proclaimed as the free response to God's gift in her, welcomed in her condition of absolute virginity (see Luke 1:26–38). That "I know not man" resonates at the beginning as the yearning and promise of wanting to know only God, only His love, anticipating in our earthly state the eschatological destiny of the sons of God. God begins to be everything in her within time (He is the Alpha and the Omega, Beginning and End) so that, through her virginity, He could be everything in us.

At the wedding of Cana, she is the one who preempts the embarrassment of the newlyweds by noticing the shortage of wine, but above all, she anticipates the manifestation of God's Kingdom with her maternal intercession in the miracle of the wine performed by Christ. She brings to fulfillment the "hour" of the Son, inaugurating the time of His public revelation to the people, until the time she accompanies Him to the crowning "hour" of Calvary where, as Mother of the covenant, she is proclaimed our Mother (see John 2:1–11; 19:25–27). Moreover, in Cana, Mary becomes herself a *sign* of the fulfillment of the Father's will. The Mother always does the Father's will, just like the Son, whose very food is the Father's will (see John 4:34). The Son obeys the Mother because in so doing, He carries out the Father's salvific will. Mary is therefore the sign of the Father's will in Christ. God's Kingdom, where God's will is at work, begins and unfolds in her and for her.

The Virgin Mary is even present in the nascent Church, where she gathers her children in unity, anticipating and realizing the mystery of the Church-communion, the call to go to all humankind and unify all peoples into one new people, the Church. Mary prefigures the virgin mother Church[154] that welcomes in her womb every new son reborn "from water and spirit" (John 3:5). In Mary's maternal virginity, the Church is reborn from on high so she (the Church) can behold the Kingdom of God (see John 3:3).

God's Kingdom, therefore, begins in her, in the novelty of her life; it is proclaimed through her; and with her, it can be fulfilled, provided that her virginity, which enfolds the Gospel message with perpetual newness like a mantle, remains inviolate. Newness in the truth, and perpetuity in the discontinuity of ages and times, can be safeguarded in the Church so long as we maintain an unshakable faith in the one who is Ever-Virgin, with whom Christ and the Church spring forth. Christ begins in her as does the Church in Christ. To possess the truth of Christ and of the Church, we must therefore safeguard the truth of Mary's mystery.

The virginity of the Mother of God is like the purest halo that protects Mary from all attempts to demean her as a mere human creature, while in turn she protects the Church and the entire Christian truth from being reduced to a mere message of human liberation or a simple social message.

Mary's virginity as the virginal womb of the Church is the root and proper understanding of Christ's proclamation, of the message that addresses, on one hand, those that have become eunuchs for the Kingdom of Heaven and, on the other, those that, living in marriage, must direct their mind to the things of God, to the things of the Kingdom, where all shall live as angels of God. Mary's virginity therefore offers an organic vision of the Church in which the primacy of the Spirit is affirmed, and thereby also a hierarchy in the states of perfection, since they are all guided by the Holy Spirit. The foundational mystery of Mary's virginity gives us a proper understanding of the Church and of the correct distinction and complementarity within her between ministry and charism. The ministry is at the service of charism, and charism is a gift for the Church's ministry and at her service, without any dissensions or pretense.

Above all, we must safeguard the "virgin truth" of Christ: what Christ has accomplished, as opposed to what we would wish for, thereby diluting His message into a sea of human words. Mary is the "virgin truth" of Christ and of the Church.

THE KINGDOM OF GOD

Our Lord's messianic ministry takes place with the proclamation of the Kingdom of God, which St. Matthew refers to as the Kingdom of Heaven to avoid pronouncing God's holy name. St. Mark tells us that Jesus begins to preach the Gospel of God by announcing, "The time is accomplished, and the kingdom of God is at hand: repent, and believe the gospel" (Mark 1:15). Therefore, "it is clear that the entire message of Jesus and the disciples consists in the announcement of the Kingdom of God. The evangelion is nothing other than the 'good news' of the Kingdom of God."[155]

Now we may ask ourselves: What is this Kingdom of God, heart of the Christian message? "The Kingdom of God is, by definition, the kingship, or sovereignty of God, and therefore all the qualities that define and describe Him match this essential attribute."[156]

Jesus fully accomplishes in His own person every expectation of the Kingdom of God. The Kingdom of God in Mark 9:1 coincides with the Son of Man and His Reign (cf. Matt. 16:28). More than that, the

Kingdom of God comes in the person of Christ. As Origen says, Christ is the *autobasileia*, the Kingdom in person.[157] This explains why subsequently the New Testament does not refer much to the "kingdom." It has a substitute in the words: "Our Lord Jesus Christ." The Church, which is the post-Resurrection continuation of Christ, continues to believe in, and announce, the Kingdom of God proclaimed by Christ without replacing it.[158]

It is therefore important always to distinguish clearly between the Kingdom of God and the Church: they are not identical, but they are not opposed to one another either. The Church is the announcement of the Kingdom of God as the sacramental continuation of Christ, and she is at the same time Christ who continues to announce His Kingdom in our midst. The Church is the key to the Kingdom.[159] Moreover, God's sovereignty is announced by Jesus. "For Him always signifies God's eschatological sovereignty....We say that Jesus' message is eschatological not because of the eschatological notion it contains (which was also present in the Prophets and in late-Judaism), but rather and above all for its very own character as an eschatological event: the Sovereignty of God has drawn closer."[160]

One can already see the time of salvation in Jesus's preaching and deeds.[161] Our Lord Jesus, therefore, is the heart of this Kingdom of God, the Son that the Father has sent into this world (see John 5:36–37).

For her part, the Virgin Mother, treasuring God's work in her heart in view of the Son, through the mystery of her perpetual virginity, proclaims in Christ God's sovereignty over everything; over even the closest human ties, which are those of flesh and blood. We could say that Mary's virginity is the most intimate perfection and grafting of God's Kingdom into a creature, enabled by God's gift, becomes daughter, spouse, and mother of the new people that Christ has come to raise by proclaiming God's Kingdom.

Mary is always turning to Christ; she reaches out to Him and welcomes within herself the Word made flesh, who is both the seed of the Kingdom and its definitive fulfillment. Mary's virginity is the assurance of the realization of the Kingdom of God, of its engraftment into human hearts, because at the root, there is a virgin heart completely open to God. Ultimately, Mary's virginity is the announcement of God's primacy, of His sovereignty over man, of His Kingdom in this world yet projected towards its ultimate end in eternal Life. Mary is, in a sense, God's eternity cast in time: the Eternal Father's self-abasement into finite time, while still abiding in timeless eternity, shines in her. Indeed, Mary's virginity points precisely to this eternity that enters time while remaining eternity: to God who becomes man without ever ceasing to be God, to God who wants us to be with Him for all eternity.

MARY'S VIRGINITY AND LIFE ACCORDING TO THE SPIRIT (CF. ROM. 8:4; GAL. 5:25)

A final aspect that we can draw attention to when describing the relationship between Mary's virginity and the Kingdom of God is one that is strictly personal and existential. The mystery of Mary's virginity is the assurance of the incarnation of God's Kingdom in our own life, until every *I* is made into an *us* in communion with God and among ourselves within the only Body of Christ, which is the Church, through the Holy Spirit given to us.

If the Kingdom of God means welcoming Christ and His sovereignty into our life so we can become His members, then Mary's virginity is that fertile terrain for God that allows His Word, the seed of the Kingdom, to blossom within us. Just as the divine seed found in her a fruitful and untainted field for bringing forth the Incarnation of the Word; in the same way, if the Virgin Mother is active within us, in the mystery of her perpetual virginity, then God's Word can also become incarnate within us. The Ever-Virgin Mary opens us up to the action of God in His Spirit and makes us live according to the Spirit. At the Annunciation, she was indissolubly united to the Holy Spirit, having been overshadowed by Him. From her and through her, the light of the Spirit extends also to us. In practice, this demands that we live in union with Mary so that through her, we can be made fruitful by the Spirit. In this way, we can live no longer as sensual beings but as spiritual beings (*pneumatikòi*), to the point where we think like Christ, which means we live fully in Him (cf. 1 Cor. 2:15).

Consequently, Mary's virginity, as the proper hermeneutic of the Kingdom of God, becomes in the Church the light that illumines the different states of Christian life by preserving above all charity as the immaculate love and by shining the light of truth on the choice of consecrated virginity and priestly celibacy on one hand and marriage on the other. The Virgin Mary drives every vocation, every choice upwards, towards "the things that are above" (Col. 3:1). Through her virginity, re-proposed in the ideal of celibate and religious life, Mary moves every soul to raise its gaze to God, her Son.

Often the temptation towards a drying up of our vocation, and a weakening of our yearning for holiness, makes itself felt in the hardships of daily life. One of the most frequent temptations, behind which lurks the venomous trickery of the devil, is precisely that of falling back onto ourselves, whereby we lose sight of the absolute good that we need to attain in the eschatological Kingdom. The Virgin protects us from this very threat, moving our yearning towards holiness and directing each vocation towards its proper end of sanctification.

These days, the errant ways of the world are trying to undermine the theological and ecclesiological importance of celibacy as a radical choice and preference for the sole love of God. In such a time, we must revive the significance of Mary's virginity in our life, and principally in that of her priestly sons. As we have discussed at length at the beginning of this book, Mary's virginity places the choice of virginity for the Kingdom of God, and of marriage, in the right order and harmony. Without doubt, virginity chosen for the Kingdom of God is superior to marriage since it brings the eschatological future towards which we are striving into the present time, allowing the realization, in the *already* of the here-and-now, of the *not yet* of the everlasting union with God who is love.

Perfection is within God and can be fully achieved in eternal life in the fully realized Kingdom. Presently, the ones that are nearest to this perfection are those already living out in their mortal flesh the spousal union of eternal love. Wherefore, we reaffirm that consecrated life is a superior state of perfection than married life. While the latter certainly also aims for Eternal Life, it does not yet live out here-and-now the *already* of the eternal condition.

As Saint Augustine says, "If the whole Church is a virgin betrothed to a man, the Christ, as we are told by the Apostle (2 Cor 11:2), what honor will not be merited by those that safeguard even in their body the integrity that all believers hold in the faith?"[162]

If we take a closer look at Jesus's stance in Matthew (19:11–12), we realize that the Kingdom of God always takes precedence and, consequently, that virginity chosen for the Kingdom excels over other vocations since it expresses in one's own flesh the Kingdom's indubitable requirement: to belong totally to Christ. In fact, our Lord:

> In proclaiming the vocation to virginity... does not directly remark on the disciples' "reaction," and neither does He remain trapped by their "reasoning": *"If the case of a man with his wife be so, it is not expedient to marry."* He appeals to another principle: the principle of the Kingdom of Heaven. It is the unique worth of the Kingdom of God that originates and illumines the choice of continence, a

choice that needs to be "personally discovered and embraced as one's own vocation." Only the singular and ineffable "treasure" of the Kingdom can "seduce" man to the point of asking of him his unmitigated self-giving through virginity."[163]

In this way, consecrated virginity, whose archetype and cause[164] is Mary's virginity—to Her we trace back this honor—illumines Matrimony in a fundamental way, urging it toward the spiritual dimension of the Kingdom's fulfillment, where in heaven there will no longer be husbands and wives but angels (cf. Mark 12:25). In turn, Matrimony illumines consecrated virginity by transposing into the present time its perseverance, replete with joys and sorrows, until the finality of its unique and indissoluble love.[165] The love of spouses, in their reciprocal support, becomes truly everlasting, venturing towards that perpetual eternity whose afterglow is resplendent in Mary's virginal love, in the mystery of the Virgin Mother. The love of consecrated souls becomes the driving force of the Church towards the fulfillment of the Kingdom, showing to everyone that God's love surpasses all understanding, that God's love is the plenitude of being. Above and beyond everything else, there is charity.

Mary Ever-Virgin is the key for a proper hermeneutic of the states of life and for the right understanding of the charisms of the Church that have been bestowed for the sanctification of all of Christ's followers.

The Virgin is she who has "seduced" God and has welcomed Him in her womb. Once again, she can seduce contemporary man by showing him the plenitude of love that is achievable in virginal consecration or in celibacy chosen for love of Christ and the Church rather than for secular or political reasons. Only she can point to the true love that in marriage strives for everlasting eternity rather than for the passing moment. The Virgin shows to the Church the way of perfect charity and accompanies her on this journey.

Epilogue

"Solus enim omnia ex natis de foemina sanctus Dominus
Jesus, qui terrenae contagia corruptelae immaculati
partus novitate non senserit . . . eo quod solus
sanctae Ecclesiae virginis, ad generandos populos Dei,
immaculatae foecunditatis aperiret genitale secretum"[166]

*O*UR STUDY HAS BEEN
directed primarily at revisiting the
beauty, sanctity, and theological neces-
sity of the Virgin Mother's mystery in a time of great
discord—the revival of the subjectivism of past years
and of objections of bygone days. We have tried primarily to present the unity between Scripture and the
sensus fidei concerning the authoritative and perennial
affirmation of Mary's perpetual virginity.

Most of all, we wanted to point out the rationality
and reasonableness of Mary's virginity in Scripture,
interpreted *sub ductu Ecclesiae* and within the broader
theological framework, where Mariology is invoked as
the golden thread that harmoniously links christology,
ecclesiology, and eschatology. Mary is she who *unifies*
because, for us, she has united heaven and earth, God
and man, the Church and the world. With St. Augustine, we have said that this unity is accomplished in
her virginal womb. Discarding the integral mystery

of her virginity to open recklessly the door to a dialogue with the world ends up diluting the Faith, while at the same time the world is alarmingly distancing itself from the Church, seeing in her merely a poor copy of itself, a simple echo-chamber of news that people want to hear. Mary shows us the truth of the Kingdom of Heaven, safeguarding ever new within herself this long-established truth.

The mystery of Mary's virginity is a gift for us. It is a mystery that unfolds itself in the Church as the opportunity for the Holy Spirit to work in us to make us holy and spotless in charity in the eyes of God (cf. Eph. 1:4).

Thus writes St. Augustine, "She [Mary] was rightly filled with so much dignity that she passed Christ onto us, preserving also her integrity, so that by faith we could conceive Him in our pure hearts and somehow through the profession of faith bring Him to light."[167]

Through her, we can conceive and bring Christ forth in our life. Without her perpetual virginity, we would be unable to participate in Christ's generation within us: it would always be a conception and birth tainted by flesh and blood. But, as the Lord warns us, flesh is of no help here, for it is the Spirit that gives life. For Mary, Christ's words always resonate as spirit and life (cf. John 6:64). Through her, Christ's words become spirit and life in us, as they do in her womb. Only if we safeguard the ever-virginity of Mary as her integral mystery can the Kingdom become spirit and life in us and through us. Otherwise, we run the risk of weakening the proclamation of the Kingdom or of transforming the Gospel into a convenient life program that basks in the splendor of the world.

If we lose Mary's virginity, the states of Christian life get muddled, overlap one another, and can even cancel each other out. Marriage then becomes superior to religious life and religious life less demanding than marriage, whereby a putative liberty of the spirit would entice the religious to discard easily their professed vows or to reduce them to mere "symbols of love." Quite soon however — it did not take long to get to this point — both marriage and the religious life degrade and fall apart, which is precisely what is happening right before our eyes. Pastoral plans and solutions will not be enough to revive them if the name of the game is still to "embrace the world" and to see the world idealistically as the "place of encounter."

If virginity/chastity is no longer essential for the *sequela Christi*, then we simply lose the notion of the Kingdom of Heaven and, with it, our own Catholic identity, the life according to the Spirit. The ultimate consequence of this is amorphism, or the absence of any form. It really does seem as if we have fallen into a void, a gloomy and deformed absence of anything. Especially the absence of beauty in the Christian proposition and its focus not on mere works but on being like Christ in accordance with His Mother, whose countenance and form resembles Him most closely.

We must revive the faith in Mary's virginity and give precedence to our heavenly Mother. The *Semper*

Virgo precedes and prepares the Church and her salvific proclamation. Gazing at her, we get unity and
order in the profession of faith and in the moral life.
If we imitate her, we return to the archetype that
bestows form to the union of virginity and spousal love. It is a union that can become the union of
virginity and the witness of martyrdom to the very
end, to the total giving of one's all in exchange for
the All. With the primeval Marian form, there will
no longer be competition between the states of life
but a hierarchical complementarity, where the end
ordains the means and not the other way round.

It seems to us also that Mary's virginity, in its three
temporal moments — *ante, in,* and *post-partum* —
runs parallel to the mystery of the Kingdom of God
in its *prelude* within her motherly womb, in its
announcement, and in its *fulfillment.* Mary's virginity
ante-partum recalls the preparation of the Kingdom's
announcement. The secretiveness of Mary's heart
that safeguarded primarily the promise of remaining
forever virgin was already a prelude to the messianic
proclamation of the Kingdom, whose echoes revealed
themselves precisely in the silence of Nazareth.

From here, by way of a revelatory manifestation,
we move to Christ's proclamation as Messiah, which
officially inaugurates the announcement of the Kingdom at the Jordan and Cana. It seems that this can
be matched with the mystery of Mary's virginity *in
partu* — namely, that seal of God that comes forth
from the enclosed womb and announces that He is
God-with-us. The virginity during the birth is like

a seal on the truth of the Kingdom — namely, the presence of God-with-us — so we can become His, as opposed to a mere longing for social emancipation.

Finally, the announcement of the Kingdom reaches out towards its definitive eschatological fulfillment in the *forever* of God. Mary as "perpetual virgin" invokes the finality of the Kingdom of Heaven. As the Ever-Virgin, Mary announces the eternal fulfillment of God's Kingdom, inviting us to stretch towards our definitive being with God for all eternity. As the "perpetual virgin," Mary echoes God, the "eternal love." God the eternal love and Mary eternally virgin: here are the wonders that God has accomplished in her. When we look at her, we can be truly hopeful. Yes, because an amorphous Christianity, without identity, self-absorbed, which welcomes everyone except true believers, now threatens to establish itself and dispel the form, every form. We must put the "virginal womb" in which the Son of God took form back at the center of the discourse.

"May Christ, son of the Virgin and
spouse of virgins, born in the flesh from
a virginal womb, mystically married
with virginal nuptials, help us."[168]
Amen.

"Hail O Lady, Holy Queen,
Holy Mother of God,
who are the Virgin
made Church."[169]

Always a Virgin

Quel nome che il cor inebria
Su di Ciel ammantato
E di belta' rallegra
Ogn'or sia per sempre amato.[170]

"ALWAYS" AND "VIRGIN," two words that in you, Mother, become one word, become your person. You are forever virgin. Time found its plenitude in you by "shrinking;" it stopped because fulfillment had occurred and then it became the abode of the Eternal One. The *always* of God, of He who is from the beginning and for evermore, descended into your virginal being. And, in this descent of God into you, you have been raised high, into His *forever*. God is in you; God is for you. You have been made virgin forever; you are the Ever-Virgin. Seal of His love, Mother of our God.

Your virginity is the expression of time meeting God, of God entering time. Your being virgin is the condition for the Eternal One to enter time so that our time could become the gateway to eternity. Time, the dimension of man, our world, the space that surrounds us, has been indwelt by God for you, because of you, through your inviolate womb. You are God's gateway into time, for you are God's time for us, O Mary! Your virginity is the *forever* of God who became man for us in time. The cradle of God. The womb of real things. The beginning. Our time becomes a *forever* with God through you, in your most holy virginity, O Mother. In you, time and eternity have touched so that they are no longer apart.

Your virginity is the blazing bush that is never consumed. Overshadowed by the Holy Spirit, you live in His shadow. Christ, the new Adam, came from you, the new earth, the God-scented "virgin earth." You brought Him to light in the splendor of your unsullied virginity. Light from Light, He came into the light for you. Just as your virginity is the light that shines on the Light, O Lady of the new Creation, your flesh and your blood, kneaded with the flour of your maternal virginity, were preparing His body and His blood. They were preparing the Eucharist, through your virginity, for you, O Mother, O most blessed one.

May that inner beauty, mark of your flawlessness and of His divinity, abide in all your Son's priests that celebrate the Holy Sacrifice. May your purity enfold them, may your virginity clothe them so that they will become true ministers of that inner beauty. You kneaded His flesh and His blood. He descended into you as true God from true God and hailed from you as the Lamb of our redemption. Your virginity prepared our Sacrifice. Your virginity safeguards our salvation.

O Virgin Mother, you are the sublime pattern of the Church, her beginning here below and her fulfillment in Heaven. Turn your eyes toward the most holy Body of your Son. The Body of the Son that came forth from you is the Church. May this mystical Body, created in your womb and brought to light on Calvary rediscover in you and in your virginity the reason for its existence. Enlighten with your inner beauty the shepherds and the faithful. Embrace all the children formed in you and for you in the image of your Son, just as the sacraments are formed in you and treasured by your virginity, especially the most Holy Eucharist.

O Ever-Virgin Mother, turn your merciful eyes toward the Church. Make the splendor of your incorruption glow incandescent in this time of loss and darkness. Show us that you are the Mother and draw all your children to your maternal heart. Show to the Church that the golden path of perfect continence for the Kingdom of Heaven, for Jesus your Son, is the way of Jesus, or rather it is Him, as He is the Way. Bestow on us a gaze of purity to contemplate the things of God and re-establish His sovereignty. Prevent us from becoming imprisoned in the arms of the world, enslaved by the ephemeral, and scattered by impurity. Give us innocent eyes to gaze at you, O Ever-Virgin. And in this way, we will be able to look straight into the eyes of God, into the eyes of the purity of God and of the Gospel. Amen.

Chaplet of Mary's Perpetual Virginity

A PRAYER FOR THE HOLINESS OF MARRIAGE, PRIESTLY CELIBACY, & CONSECRATED LIFE

As we know, the dogma of the Perpetual Virginity of our Blessed Lady is one of the four Marian dogmas of the Church, alongside the Immaculate Conception, the Assumption, and the Motherhood of our Lady.

We are grateful to Father Serafino Lanzetta for his reflections on the dogma of the Perpetual Virginity, and particularly how the dogma impacts the living out of chastity in the sacrament of Marriage, celibacy in the priesthood, and chastity as lived in Consecrated Life.

This timely booklet reveals a prayerful spiritual synthesis of Father Serafino's insights and implications for these states of life flowing from the dogma of Perpetual virginity.

Imprimatur:

✠ *Stephen Robson, Bishop of Dunkeld*

WHY A CHAPLET DEVOTED TO HONORING OUR LADY'S PERPETUAL VIRGINITY AND WHAT DOES IT CONSIST IN?

Having reached the end of our theological analysis, we wish to summarize it in the form of a prayer that can help the faithful believe ever more firmly in the dogma of Mary's perpetual virginity, and then to pray it with love and devotion. According to the law dear to Christianity, that foundational link between the *lex credendi* and the *lex orandi*, by praying, dogma becomes clearer to the intellect and is welcomed more readily by the will under the influence of grace. We believe in order to pray, and we pray in order to believe ever more fervently, in accordance with the faith of the Church.

In what follows, we present the text of a Chaplet of Mary's Perpetual Virginity. The reader will be able to evaluate its scope and effectiveness. Should the Son of the Virgin, our Lord Jesus Christ, deem it appropriate, it may then be disseminated to increase devotion among God's people.

The chaplet comprises seven mysteries that recall seven instances concerning Mary's virginity: the pre-Annunciation in the old Covenant, the realization in the new Covenant at the Annunciation, the virginity during the birth, the virginity after the birth, the virginity believed by the Church, the virginity prayed by the Church, and finally Mary's virginity as the Christ-making and Christ-forming model of the Church and of Christianity.

For every mystery, we recite the *Pater* once, the *Ave Maria* seven times, and the *Gloria Patri*, followed by the short prayer "Perpetual Virgin, pray for us."

FIRST MYSTERY
THE VIRGIN MARY IS
PRE-ANNOUNCED BY ISAIAH

"Behold a virgin shall conceive, and bear a son,
and his name shall be called Emmanuel" (Is. 7:14).

Grace of the Mystery
An unwavering faith in our Lady's perpetual virginity
and an increase in devotion to this dogma.

Act of Reparation
For the loss of faith in our Lady's perpetual virginity
and the blasphemies against this sublime mystery.

Meditation
"Always" and "virgin", two words that in you, Mother,
become one word, become your person. You are forever
virgin. Time found its plenitude in you by "shrinking";
it stopped because fulfillment had occurred and then it
became the abode of the Eternal One.

Pater Noster. Ave Maria (7×). Gloria Patri.
Perpetual Virgin, pray for us.

SECOND MYSTERY
THE VIRGIN MARY CONCEIVES JESUS BY THE POWER OF THE HOLY SPIRIT

"The Virgin's name was Mary" (Luke 1:27).

"The Holy Ghost shall come upon thee, and the power of the most High shall overshadow thee" (Luke 1:35).

Grace of the Mystery
An unwavering faith in the divinity of Jesus Christ, true God and true man.

Act of Reparation
For the weakening of our faith in the divinity of Jesus Christ, our unique source of Salvation.

Meditation
The *always* of God, of He who is from the beginning and for evermore, descended into your Virgin being. And in this descent of God into you, you have been raised high, into His *forever*. God is in you; God is for you. You have been made virgin forever, you are the Ever-Virgin, Seal of His love, Mother of our God.

Pater Noster. Ave Maria (7×). Gloria Patri.
Perpetual Virgin, pray for us.

THIRD MYSTERY
MARY GIVES BIRTH TO JESUS
VIRGINALLY AND WITHOUT SUFFERING

"The Holy which shall be born of thee shall
be called the Son of God" (Luke 1:35).

Grace of the Mystery

A reaffirming of the value of chaste, indissoluble, and
fruitful marriage, according to the Will of God.

Act of Reparation

For the sins against the sacredness of marriage and the family.

Meditation

Your virginity is the expression of time meeting God, of
God entering time. Your being virgin is the condition
for the Eternal One to enter time so that our time could
become the gateway to eternity. Time, the dimension of
man, our world, the space that surrounds us, has been
indwelt by God for you, because of you, through your
inviolate womb. You are God's gateway into time, you are
God's time for us, O Mary! Your virginity is the *forever*
of God, who became man for us in time. The cradle of
God. The womb of real things. The beginning. Our time
becomes a *forever* with God through you, in your most
holy virginity, O Mother. In you, time and eternity have
touched so that they are no longer apart.

Pater Noster. Ave Maria (7×). Gloria Patri.
Perpetual Virgin, pray for us.

FOURTH MYSTERY
MARY REMAINS A VIRGIN AFTER THE BIRTH

"I know not man" (Luke 1:34).

Grace of the Mystery

The indissolubility of priestly celibacy and a renewed appreciation for the holiness of consecrated life.

Act of Reparation

For the sins against the sacredness of the priesthood and of consecrated life.

Meditation

May that inner beauty, mark of your flawlessness and of His divinity, abide in all your Son's priests that celebrate the Holy Sacrifice. May your purity enfold them; may your virginity clothe them so that they will become true ministers of that inner beauty. You kneaded His flesh and His blood. He descended into you as true God from true God and hailed from you as the Lamb of our redemption. Your virginity prepared our Sacrifice. Your virginity safeguards our salvation.

Pater Noster. Ave Maria (7×). Gloria Patri.
Perpetual Virgin, pray for us.

FIFTH MYSTERY
*MARY'S VIRGINITY IS PROFESSED
IN THE CREED OF THE CHURCH*

"By the power of the Holy Spirit He was
born of the Virgin Mary" (*Nicene Creed*).

Grace of the Mystery

A growth in our love and reverence for our Eucharistic
Lord by receiving Holy Communion in a state of grace,
on the tongue and kneeling.

Act of Reparation

For the sacrileges against the Holy Eucharist, especially
through the practice of receiving Communion in a state
of mortal sin or with lack of reverence and adoration.

Meditation

O Virgin Mother, you are the sublime pattern of the
Church, her beginning here below and her fulfillment in
Heaven. Turn your eyes toward the most holy Body of your
Son. The Body of the Son that came forth from you is the
Church. May this mystical Body, created in your womb and
brought to light on Calvary, rediscover in you and in your
virginity the reason for its existence. Enlighten with your
inner beauty the shepherds and the faithful. Embrace all
the children formed in you and for you in the image of your
Son, just as the sacraments are formed in you and treasured
by your virginity, especially the most Holy Eucharist.

*Pater Noster. Ave Maria (7×). Gloria Patri.
Perpetual Virgin, pray for us.*

SIXTH MYSTERY:
MARY'S VIRGINITY IS
CELEBRATED BY THE CHURCH

"Your honorable virginity, O Mary, is the blazing bush
that Moses saw burning without being consumed"
(*From the Liturgy of our Lord's Circumcision*).

Grace of the Mystery
A recovery of the sense of the sacredness of the Holy Mass and
devotion to the Holy Mass according to the traditional rite.

Act of Reparation
For the liturgical abuses in the celebration of the Holy
Mass and the contempt for the uninterrupted *lex orandi*
of the Church.

Meditation
Your virginity is the blazing bush that is never consumed.
Overshadowed by the Holy Spirit, you live in His shadow.
Christ, the new Adam, came from you, the new earth, the
God-scented "virgin earth." You brought Him to light in
the splendor of your unsullied virginity. Light from Light,
He came into the light through you. Just as your virginity
is the light that shines on the Light, O Lady of the new
Creation, your flesh and your blood, kneaded with the flour
of your maternal virginity, were preparing His body and
His blood. They were preparing the Eucharist, through
your virginity, through you, O Mother, O most blessed one.

Pater Noster. Ave Maria (7×). Gloria Patri.
Perpetual Virgin, pray for us.

SEVENTH MYSTERY:
*MARY'S VIRGINITY MADE CHRIST
AND FORMS CHRIST WITHIN US*

"Hail O Lady, Holy Queen, Holy Mother of God,
Who are the virgin made Church" (*St. Francis of Assisi*).

Grace of the Mystery

The virginal purity of the Catholic Faith and the restoration
of God's sovereignty in the hearts and souls of all the faithful.

Act of Reparation

For the silent apostasy among the flock of Christ.

Meditation

O Ever-Virgin Mother, turn your merciful eyes toward the
Church. Make the splendor of your incorruption glow
incandescent in this time of loss and darkness. Show us
that you are the Mother and draw all your children to your
maternal heart. Show to the Church that the golden path
of perfect continence for the Kingdom of Heaven, for Jesus
your Son, is the way of Jesus, or rather it is Him, as He is
the Way. Bestow on us a gaze of purity to contemplate the
things of God and re-establish His sovereignty. Prevent
us from becoming imprisoned in the arms of the world,
enslaved by the ephemeral, and scattered by impurity. Give
us innocent eyes to gaze at you, O Ever-Virgin. And in this
way, we will be able to look straight into the eyes of God.
Into the eyes of the purity of God and of the Gospel.

*Pater Noster. Ave Maria (7×). Gloria Patri.
Perpetual Virgin, pray for us.*

Pray for us, O Holy Mother of God.
That we may be made worthy of the promises of Christ.

Let us pray. O God, who bestowed on men eternal salvation through the fruitful virginity of the Blessed Virgin Mary, grant us, we beseech you, to experience the intercession of she through whom we have merited to receive the Author of Life, our Lord Jesus Christ, Your Son, who with You lives and reigns in the unity of the Holy Spirit, world without end. Amen.

NOTES

FOREWORD

1 Heinrich Denzinger, *Enchiridion Symbolorum: A Compendium of Creeds, Definitions, and Declarations on Matters of Faith and Morals*, ed. Peter Hünermann (San Francisco: Ignatius Press, 2012), 1810 (Hereafter: DH); see also: Pope Pius XII, Encyclical Letter on Holy Virginity *Sacra virginitas* (March 25, 1954).

INTRODUCTION

1 "Holy Scriptures were fulfilled, when you were ineffably born of the Virgin; You came down as the dew on the fleece to save humankind: we praise Thee Our God" (From the Office of the feast *In Circumcisione Domini*).

2 Cf. St. Ambrose, *De virginibus*, 2.2.18 in *Patrologiae cursus completus, series latina* 16 (Paris: J.-P. Migne, 1841-1857; facsimile reprint, Turnhout: Brepols, 1982-1993), col. 211 (hereafter cited as *PL*).

3 Cf. St. Ambrose, *De institutione virginis*, 5.33; 17.105 in *PL* 16, coll. 313, 331.

4 St. Ambrose, *De virginibus*, 2.2.15 in *PL* 16, col. 210.

5 Cf. St. Ambrose, *De virginibus*, 1.6.31 in *PL* 16, col. 197. The virgin consecrated to God is, for St. Ambrose, a "sacrament" of the Church, its mysterious presence, just as the Church is a sacrament of Christ. The person who consecrates her virginity to Christ is a mother who welcomes all her children, gathers them together in unity, and guides them in the song of salvation, exactly as Moses's sister Mary did (see Ex. 15:20), and is also a figure also of the Church, which, with "an immaculate spirit, united the pious crowds of the people in singing the divine hymns." St. Ambrose, *De virginibus*,1.3.12 in *PL* 16, col. 192.

6 Cf. St. Ambrose, *Expositio in Lucam*, II.7 in *PL* 15, col. 1555, cited also by Vatican Council II, Dogmatic Constitution on the Church *Lumen gentium* (November 21, 1964), n. 63.

7 Cf. St. Jerome, *Letter to Pammachius*, 48.21 in *Corpus Scriptorum Ecclesiasticorum Latinorm: Epistulae 1-70*, ed. I. Hilberg, vol. 54 (Salzburg: De Gruyter, 1910), 386, (hereafter cited as *CSEL*).

8 Cf. St. Athanasius, *Sur la Virginité*, in Louis Théophile Lefort, trans., *Le Muséon* 42 (1929): 247.

9   St. Augustine, *Sermo 51*, 16.26 in *PL* 38, col. 348.

10   St. Maximus the Confessor, *The Life of the Virgin*, trans.
Stephen J. Shoemaker (New York: Yale University Press, 2012), 51. It
is the first English translation of a work originally written in Greek
but conserved only in the ancient Georgian language, attributed to
St. Maximus the Confessor (580–662), one of the most important
theologians of the Byzantine Church. The argument that Shoemaker offers in his introduction and in the annotations appear
decisive in acknowledging the authorship of St. Maximus. It is
the first biography of the Holy Virgin, which, like the *Protoevangelium,* commences with her Conception and concludes with her
Dormition and Assumption, after having extolled the Ever-Virgin
Theotokos with titles of the loftiest praises. In 1986, Michel-Jean
van Esbroeck published a French translation of the *Life of Mary*
(in *CSCO* 478–79), and he also acknowledged the authorship of
the Confessor. Shoemaker corrects several points in the preceding
translation, thus offering a text more in conformity with the original. Among the various prerogatives of our Lady, he indicates that
of her *compassion*, read as *co-redemption* and the *mediation* of grace.
There are many similarities and parallels, especially with the *Life
of Mary* written by John Geometres around 980.

11   To those Catholic theologians who allowed themselves to
be captivated by liberal Protestantism, accepting the category of
"theologoumenon" to free Christianity from mythological notions
such as the virginal conception of Jesus, Hans Urs von Balthasar
responds in this way: "Have Catholic theologians gotten so blind
they no longer see that the Virginity of Mary is entwined to the
centre of dogmatics? Or do they want to start distinguishing a
'theological' truth from a 'historical' truth in a religion that deals
no less with the Incarnation, namely the historical truth of the
pivotal substance of the Faith?" Hans Urs von Balthasar, *Cordula,
ovverosia il caso serio* (Brescia: Editrice Queriniana, 1968), 84.

12   "Quid dicis Iudæe, quid proponis, quid astruis, quid obi-
cis, quid obiectas? Ecce virgo nostra ex stirpe tua est, ex genere
tua est, ex radice tua est, ex traduce tua est....Verumtamen ex
fide nostra est, ex credulitate nostra est, ex adsensu nostra est, ex
reverentia nostra est, ex honorificentia nostra est, ex laude nostra
est, ex glorificatione nostra est, ex dilectione nostra est, ex amore
nostra est, ex prædicatione nostra est, ex præconio nostra est, ex
defensione nostra est, ex vindicatione nostra est. Quod enim tibi
[to the People elect] Spiritus Sanctus de illa per prophetas dixit, per

oracula intimavit, per figuras innotuit, per præcedentia promisit, per subsequentia complevit, te negante, te non credente, te respuente, te abnuente, te resultante, te blasphemante, ego novi, ego credidi, ego sapio, ego venero, ego honoro, ego glorifico, ego amplecto, ego diligo, ego prædico, quia me gratia prævenit, fides implevit.... Si enim ut ais, iuvencula et non virgo parere posset, quid significaret Dominus? quid miraculi daret, quid admirabile demonstraret, quid inusitatem ostenderet." St. Ildefonsus of Toledo, *De virginitate Sanctae Mariae*, ed. V. Yarza Urquiola, *Corpus Christianorum Series Latina*, vol. 114A (Turnhout, Belgium: Brepols Publishing, 2007), 165–67, (hereafter cited as *CCSL*). St. Ildefonsus (+ 667), master of the faith, "exercised great influence on Marian literature in Spain, in particular by defending the perpetual Virginity of Our Most Blessed Lady, in a special way against the Jews who kept opposing Christians."Stefano M. Manelli, *La Mariologia nella storia della Salvezza: Sintesi storico-teologica: Eta' medievale, Immaculata Mediatrix* 2.3 (2002): 286 [285-322]; Stefano M. Manelli, *La Mariologia nella storia della Salvezza: Sintesi storico-teologica* (Frigento: Casa Mariana Editrice, 2014), 106, 117.

13 St. Augustine, *Sermo 192:In Natale Domini*,, 2 in *PL* 38, coll. 1012–13.

14 St. Maximus the Confessor, *The Life of the Virgin*, 156.

CHAPTER I

15 St. Jerome, *Epistula 43 ad Pammachium*, 21. "Christ is virgin, virgin is Mary, of both sexes they have consecrated the origins of virginity."

16 Origen, commenting on this excerpt from the Gospel of Mathew (19:21), writes that "he who has exchanged his riches for poverty in order to be perfect, does not become completely perfect the moment he gives away his possessions to the poor; however, from that day forward the contemplation of God begins disposing him towards every virtue." Cited by St. Thomas Aquinas, *Summa Theologica*, II-II, q. 186, a. 1.

17 "It is said explicitly that one is in a state of perfection not because his act of charity is perfect, but because he undertakes perpetually, with a certain solemnity, that which pertains to perfection.... Consequently, nothing prevents there being some perfect [people] who are not in the state of perfection; and on the contrary that there are some in the state of perfection who are not perfect." Aquinas, *Summa Theologica*, II-II, q. 184, a. 4. See also

Aquinas, *Summa Theologica*, II-II, q. 186, a. 1, ad 4: "The religious state was instituted principally to acquire perfection by means of practical acts to eliminate the obstacles that oppose perfect charity. By eliminating these obstacles, the occasions of sin (which totally destroys charity) are radically excluded."

18   Both the Greek text of 1 Corinthians and the version of the Septuagint for Genesis render the expression "a good thing" with the adjective *kalòs*.

19   The expression *meinosin os kago* referred to the unmarried and widows called on to "remain" like St. Paul implies that he himself "remained" unmarried. Since the time of Luther, the celibacy of St. Paul has been challenged. Many Fathers maintain that the Apostle was never married, albeit Clement of Alexandria (*Stromateis*, 3:53:I) claimed to have found a reference to the Apostle's wife in "*gnésie syzyge*" of Philippians 4:3, as *syzygos* in the feminine means "wife" in classic, Hellenistic Greek. See Richard Kugelman, "The First Letter to the Corinthians," in Raymond Brown, Joseph Fitzmyer, Ronald Murphy, *The Jerome Biblical Commentary* (London: Geoffrey Chapman, 1974), 263. Many interpreters maintain — with regards to the letter to the Philippians — that St. Paul was referring in reality to diverse associates in the work of the Gospel. Since the word is found among three proper names (Evodia, Syntyche, and Clement), it is even more correct to assume that *syzyke* is instead a proper name. See Joseph Henry Thayer, *Greek-English Lexicon of the New Testament and Other Early Christian Literature*, n. 4805.

20   See Stefano M. Manelli, *Mariologia biblica* (Casa Mariana Editrice: Frigento, 2005), 141–48, in which the author agrees with the perspective of A. Vincent Cernuda, quoted also by René Laurentin — namely, that St. Paul must have known that Christ was born virginally by the Mother, although this does not constitute a preeminent characteristic of Pauline theology, the concise allusion reveals two fundamental things: the taking of a tangible humanity and its virginal realization. In addition, according to Father Manelli, in agreement with other important authors, in this Pauline text you can discern not only the *virginal maternity* of Mary but also her *divine maternity* in relation to the Son of God ("God sent His Son" Gal. 4:4) and of her *spiritual maternity* in relation to the adopted sons of God ("that we might receive the adoption of sons" Gal. 4:5). English version of Fr Stefano Manelli's *All Generations Shall Call Me Blessed: Biblical Mariology* (New Bedford, MA: Academy of the Immaculate, 2005).

21 Pius XII, apostolic constitution *Provida Mater Ecclesia* (February 2, 1947), no. 6.

22 Pius XII, *Provida Mater Ecclesia*, no. 9.

23 Pius XII, *Ibid.*, no. 9.

24 Vatican Council II, dogmatic constitution *Lumen gentium* (November 21, 1964), no. 43.

25 Vatican Council II, *Lumen gentium*, no. 43.

26 See can. 588§1.

27 Can. 574§1.

28 John Paul II, apostolic exhortation *Vita consecrata* (March 25, 1996), no. 1.

29 John Paul II, *Ibid.*, no. 35.

30 See also the accurate sociological analysis by Father Ángel Pardilla, *La realtà della vita religiosa: Analisi e bilancio di cinquant'anni (1965-2015) e prospettive* (Rome: LEV, 2016). This study highlights that in the fifty years analyzed, from the end of Vatican II until today, religious institutes and societies of apostolic life for men recorded a drop of 39.58 percent, corresponding to a loss of 130,545 members. While the institutes and societies for women recorded a drop of 44.61 percent corresponding to the loss of 428,828 members. The religious institute that suffered the gravest exodus was the Jesuits, which lost 53.54 percent of its members. The Friars Minor follow with 49.5 percent, the Benedictines with 42.2 percent, and the Salesians with 30.72 percent. What happened? Father Pardilla indicates two causes: the inadequate and defective receptivity of the Vatican II documents on religious life and of the apostolic exhortation *Vita consecrata*. Whether this is sufficient to map out the roots of the grave crisis may certainly be up for discussion.

31 Cf. Ma Isabel Ardanza Mendilibar, *La riduzione: tempo di grazia per vivere la fede,* in *La vita religiosa come esodo UISG* n. 154 (2014): 22.

32 J. Arregui, *Atteggiamenti per vivere cambiando,* in *La vita religiosa come esodo,* 24.

33 Antonio M. Sicari, "Matrimonio e verginità nella problematica della Tradizione," *Ephemerides Carmeliticae* 28.2 (1977): 226–77.

34 "What should have been defended at that time was not so much the right to the existence of celibacy or continence (this was evident for Christians at that time), but more the right for a Christian to matrimony. The sentiment underpinning this attitude may be described as follows: matrimony, a blessing of creation (even if degraded in its sexuality by sin), is intended for those Christians

who are unable to practice continence. This appears clear, moreover, in the patristic use of the biblical term: 'Bride of Christ.' By the mere reality of Baptism, every believer is included in this spousal relationship which, beginning since the time of Origen, has been extended to all the faithful individually. Gradually, however, this term has been reserved only for 'virgins consecrated to God' and in the IV century this application was by then an accepted fact. In this way the believer, who for the love of God did not marry, became the typical Christian, a notion whose formulation was to cast a shadow on the full worthiness of matrimony, as follows: matrimony, at any rate matrimony with the sexual relation (patristics acknowledged also matrimony in continence), came to be considered a respectable way out for the weaker Christians." Edward Schillebeeckx, *Il celibato del ministero ecclesiatico* (Roma: Edizioni Paoline, 1968), 33–34, cit. in *ivi*, 234–35.

35   Schillebeeckx, *Il celibato del ministero ecclesiatico*, 33–34, cit. in *ivi*, 238.

36   Schillebeeckx, *Ibid.*, 33–34, cit. in *ivi*, 246.

37   Schillebeeckx, *Ibid.*, 33–34, cit. in *ivi*, 247.

38   Schillebeeckx, *Ibid.*, 33–34, cit. in *ivi*, 271.

39   Schillebeeckx, *Ibid.*, 33–34, cit. in *ivi*, 277.

40   His studies on this theme are *Zur Theologie der Entsagung*, in *Orientierung*, 17 (1953): 252–55; *Über die evangelischen Räte*, in *Geist und Leben*, 37 (1964): 17–34.

41   According to Karl Rahner, marriage as sanctified life, totally incarnated in time and history, corresponds to the mystery of the incarnation — namely, to the presence of Christ in the world — while virginity in a strict sense — e.g., physical — and religious life in its broad sense as consecrated life by evangelical counsels is assigned to the eschatology (the afterlife).

42   Cf. Richard Kugelman, *The First Letter to the Corinthians*, 265.

43   Hans Urs von Balthasar, *The Christian State of Life* (San Francisco: Ignatius, 1994).

44   See Paul O'Callaghan's position, which is an exemplar of *Opus Dei*, "The States of Life for a Christian: Reflections on a Work by Hans Urs von Balthasar," *Annales Theologici* 21 (2007): 61–100.

45   See Hans Urs von Balthasar, *The States of Life for a Christian*, 86, 103.

46   "In fact, the religious undertake a vow to refrain from the goods of the world, which they would have been able to use

legitimately, in order to attend to God with greater freedom: *and in this the perfection of the present life consists.*" St. Thomas Aquinas, *Summa Theologica* II-II, q. 185, a. 5 (emphasis added).

47 Please refer to some of my reflections in this regard, so far only sketched out and in need of further study: Serafino M. Lanzetta, *Il mistero dell'unione sponsale con Dio, Fides Catholica* 9.2 (2016): 179–95.

48 "*Memento Domine orthodoxorum presbyterorum, omnisque ordinis diaconici et ministerii omniumque virginitate servantium et omnis fidelissimi populi tui.*" Cipriano Vagaggini, *The Canon of the Mass and Liturgical Reform* (Geoffrey Chapman: London, 1967), 56. This addresses St. Basil's typical Greek-Alexandrian anaphora, with reference to the Antiochene model. Hieronymus Engberding demonstrated that this anaphora is more ancient than the Byzantine one, which also carries St. Basil's name. *Das Eucharistische Hochgebet der Basileiosliturgie* (Münster: Aschendorff, 1931). Cf. Vagaggini, *The Canon of the Mass and Liturgical Reform*, 49–50.

49 Pius XII, encyclical letter *Sacra virginitas* (March 25, 1954), AAS 46 (1954): 161 [161–91].

50 Pius XII, *Sacra virginitas*, AAS 46 (1954): 174.

51 St. Augustine, *Epistola 167, PL* 33. St. Augustine synthesized Jovinian's errors as follows: "Not many years ago in Rome a certain Jovinian pushed for the '*sanctimoniales*' even of an advanced age to marry, not by appealing to pleasure... but by arguing that before God there is no difference in the merit of the '*virgines sanctimoniales*' and that of those married." *De peccatorum meritis et remissione* 3, 7.13, in *PL* 44, col. 193.

52 See the defense made by St. Jerome in his treatise against the monk Jovinian, especially in *Letter 48 to Pammachius* (*CSEL* 54, 350–87). Pammachius and other friends had refused to publish the treatise that St. Jerome had sent to them in Rome, maintaining that the author had exaggerated in exalting virginity at the expense of Matrimony. This letter was written in 393 or 394.

53 St. Jerome, *Contro Gioviniano*, 1.3, in *PL* 23, col. 223.

54 St. Jerome, *Contro Gioviniano*, 1.32 in *PL* 23, col. 266. St. Jerome had at first dwelled on the meaning of *almah*, with which Isaiah renders the word "virgin." In fact, *almah*, St. Jerome explains, does not mean "virgin" but "young woman." "Virgin" is rendered with *bethulah*. However, even more precisely, "young woman" or "maiden" (for the married state), St. Jerome tells us, is rendered in Hebrew by *naarah*. What then does *almah* mean? It means "hidden

virgin," namely, a girl who is not only a virgin but is a virgin and something else, given that not every virgin is hidden or far from the occasion of meeting a man. Rebecca, St. Jerome explains, by virtue of her extreme purity and being a figure of the Church, is described in Genesis 24:43 as *almah* and not *bethulah*. With these considerations, St. Jerome tells us that the Holy Spirit did not choose a "married woman" (albeit the Virgin Mary was already married to Joseph), but a "hidden virgin," the quintessential figure of the Church.

55   The proposal of *Amoris laetitia* is to admit to Holy Communion couples who live in an irregular situation — i.e, divorced and remarried — after a period of discernment, as if the discernment were a slight of hand to make suddenly that *more uxorio* union sacramentally valid.

56   See St. Jerome, *Letter XXII to Eustachia* in *PL* 22,394–425 and *Against Jovinian* I,3, in *PL* 23,223

57   The Ebionites were a Judaizing Christian sect; their main characteristic was an extreme attachment to the law. They challenged Mary's virginity, maintaining that Christ was the natural son of Joseph and his spouse. St. Jerome attests to their existence at the end of the fourth century.

CHAPTER 2

58   From the Office for the feast *In Circumcisione Domini*. "In the burning bush that Moses saw without being consumed, we acknowledge your laudable virginity: O Holy Mother of God intercede for us."

59   Cf. *Chronicon Paschale, Patrologiae Cursus Completus, Series Graeca*, ed. Jacques-Paul Migne, vol. 92 (Paris: 1857-1866) coll. 1335–48 (hereafter cited as *PG*).

60   See Aristotle, *Physica* A.7.190b 20; B, 2, 194b 35; *Metaphysica* V.2.1013b; *De Anima* II.1.412a 8–9.

61   See Aristotle, *Metaphysica* IX.8.1050a.

62   See Aristotle, *De Anima* II.1.412a 10; *Metaphysica* II.1.993b 24–31; *Metaphysica* V.4.1015a.

63   Frequently, when Aristotle speaks of "form," he puts together the two terms *morphe* and *eidos* with the purpose of going beyond the concept of form or Plato's separate idea (*eidos*). See Ronald Polansky, *Aristotle's* De Anima: *A Critical Commentary* (New York: Cambridge University Press, 2007), 148.

64   Martin Mosebach, *The Heresy of Formlessness: The Roman Liturgy and its Enemy* (Brooklyn, NY: Angelico Press, 2018).

65 "*Sicut humanam illam formam ex virgine Maria Trinitas operata est sed solius Filii persona est, visibilem namque Filii solius personam invisibilis Trinintas operata est.*" St. Augustine, *De Trinitate* II, 10.18 in *PL* 42, col. 857. The official Italian translation renders "*humanam illam formam*" with "human nature"; the English with "Human form."

66 St. Augustine, *Sermo* 72/A, 7 in *PL* 46, col. 937.

67 St. Augustine, *Ibid.*.

68 Here, Father Manelli refers to St. Louis de Montfort, *A Treatise on True Devotion to the Blessed Virgin*, nos. 219–21 and *The Secret of Mary*, nos. 16–18.

69 Stefano Manelli, *Maria Santissima nella Vita Spirituale: Trattato di Spiritualita' mariana* (Frigento: Casa Mariana Editrice, 2017), 158.

70 Cf. G. Besutti, "Litanie," in *Nuovo Dizionario di Mariologia*, ed. Stefano De Fiores and Salvatore Meo (Milano: Edizioni paoline, Cinisello Balsamo, 1985), 759–60.

71 For example, the list offered by Andrea Gianetti Luis, *Rosario della Sacratissima Vergine Maria* (Venetia: Appresso Bernardo Giunti, 1587), 140.

72 For this liturgical text, and for the one following, see the *Breviarium Romanum*, editio prima iuxta typicam, 1960. Also, the hymn for the Lauds of the Octave of the Nativity is very significant. We shall indicate only two verses befitting our theme: "*Domus pudici pectoris, Templum repente fit Dei; Intacta nesciens virum, Verbo concepit alvo Filium. / Enititur puerpera, Quem Gabriel praedixerat, Quem ventre matris gestiens, Baptistas clausus senserat.* English translation: "The mansion of the modest breast suddenly becomes a shrine where God shall rest: pure and undefiled, she conceives in her womb the Son. That Son, that royal Son she bore, whom Gabriel's voice had told afore: whom, in His Mother yet concealed, the Infant Baptist had revealed." It is significant here to reflect on the verse, "*Quem matris gestiens, Clausus Ioannes senserat*" in relation to the presence of the Blessed Virgin with child visiting Elizabeth. In a very eloquent passage, St. Maximus the Confessor ascribes to Elizabeth, in the mystery of the Visitation, acknowledgment of our Lady's virginal conception by the work of the Holy Spirit, who inspires her words: "*Blessed art Thou among women and blessed is the fruit of Thy womb!*" (Luke 1:42). Cf. St. Maximus the Confessor, *The Life of the Virgin*, trans. Stephen J. Shoemaker (New Haven, CT: Yale University Press, 2012), 56.

73 Very significant, and in high praise of Mary's virginity consecrated by her miraculous motherhood, is also the Secret on the feast
of the Nativity of the Blessed Virgin Mary: "*Unigeniti tui, Domine,
nobis succurrat humanitas : ut, qui natus de Virgine, matris integritatem non minuit, sed sacravit; in Nativitatis ejus solemniis nostris,
nos piaculis exuens, oblationem nostram tibi faciat acceptam Jesus
Christus Dominus noster.* English translation: "May the humanity
of thy only begotten Son succor us, O Lord: that Jesus Christ our
Lord, who, when born of a Virgin, did not lessen but did consecrate
his mother's virginity, may on this solemnity of her Nativity, deliver
us from our sins, and make our oblation, our Lord Jesus Christ,
acceptable to Thee." *Missale Romanum*, editio typicam, 1962, die 8
Septembris. "The motherhood of the blessed Virgin was the beginning of our salvation" — "*quibus beatæ Virginis partus exstit salutis
exordium*" — is the theme of the *oratio* of the same feast *In Nativitate
Beatae Mariae Virginis*. Given their antiquity (fourth century in the
East and the end of the seventh century in the West), such extracts
serve as *exemplum* for other Marian feasts: cf. *In Desponsatione B.
Mariæ V. cum Ioseph* (January 23) and also the *Feast of the Conception
of Mary*, widespread in the West since the tenth century and in the
Roman Calendar since 1476. In fact, these extracts appear already in
the British Library: *Office of the Mass for the Immaculate Conception
of the Virgin Mary for the King Henry VII*, 1485–1509.

74 St. Augustine, *Sermo 191*, 1.2 in *PL* 38, col. 1010.

75 *Ibid.*

76 *Ibid.*, 2.3 in *PL* 38, coll. 1010–11.

77 *Ibid.*, 3.4 in *PL* 38, col. 1011.

78 "She (the Church) is truly a Bride, who regenerates Christ's
new infancy with the Virgin Birth." St. Peter Chrysologous, *Sermo
146*, 5 in *PL* 52, col. 593.

79 St. Maximus the Confessor, *The Life of the Virgin*, 54.

80 *PG* 92, 1335–48.

81 Father George Papadeas translates this Marian title as "*Hail!
O Bride Ever Virgin!*" *The Akathist Hymn Preceded by the Brief
Compline*, trans. Fr. George Papadeas (Daytona Beach: Patmos Press,
1994). Cf. Luigi Gambero, *Mary and the Fathers of the Church: The
Blessed Virgin Mary in Patristic Thought* (San Francisco: Ignatius
Press, 1999), 342.

82 Gambero, *Mary and the Fathers of the Church*, 296.

83 St. Peter Chrysolog us, *Sermo 140*, 2 in *PL* 52, col. 576.
Christ is also defined by Chrysologus as "bridegroom and guardian

of the purity of his mother." *Sermo 140*, 2 in *Corpus Christianorum Latinorum* 24B, 854. See also his *Sermo 145*, 4 in *PL* 52, col. 589, in which the spousal typology of Christ with Mary is depicted with the words of *Song of Songs* 4:12.

84 The first to mention our Lady as "bride of Christ" is St. Ephraim the Syrian, *Hymn on the Nativity*, 16, 10, in *CSCO* 187, 76. Cf. Gambero, *Mary and the Fathers of the Church*, 117, with a veiled reference to Eve who was Adam's bride and still a virgin.

85 To further develop this point, chastity in marriage, as being faithful to God's plan on sexuality and procreation, is indeed an expression of a spiritual virginity that characterises the spousal love as such. The spousal love is lived out physically and spiritually in the state of virginity and spiritually only in that of marriage.

86 See V. Milazzo, "Virginity and Martyrdom: Ages in Damasus, Ambrose, and Prudentius" in *Ex Pluribus Unum: Studi in Onore di Giulia Sfameni Gasparro*, ed. C. Giuffre'Scibona and A. Mastrocinque (Rome: Quasar, 2015), 397–413.

87 *"Natalis est virginis, integritatem sequamur. Natalis est martyris, hostias immolemus."* St. Ambrose, *De virginibus*, 1.2.5 in *PL* 16, col. 189.

88 St. Ambrose, *De virginibus*, 2.6 in *PL* 16, col. 190.

89 *Ibid.*, 2.8 in *PL* 16, col. 190.

90 Origen, *Commentary on the Epistle to the Romans*, 9.1 in *PG* 14, col. 1205. He adds, "In the Church the first sacrificial offering, after that of the Apostles, is that of the martyrs, the second, that of virgins and the third, that of the celibates."

91 See *Brevarium Romanum*, edition prima iuxta typicam, 1960.

92 See H. Crouille, "rigéne, précurseur du monachisme" in *Théologie de la vie monastique: Etudes sur la Tradition patristique*, Collection *Théologie:* Etudes publiées sous la direction de la Faculté de Théologie S.J. de Lyon-Fourvière, n. 49 (Paris: Aubier, 1961), 18–21.

93 See Origen, *Homily on Numbers*, 10.2 in SCh 29, 196.

94 Cf. St. Justin Martyr, *Dialogue with Tryphus*, 100 in *PG* 6, coll. 709–12; St. Irenaeus of Lyon, *Adversus haereses*, 3.22 in *PG* 7, coll. 959–60.

95 The bibliography on this subject is very vast. Here we refer only to an important collection of studies: *Maria Co-redentrice. Storia e Teologia*, 20 vols. (Frigento: Casa Mariana Editrice, 1998–2018).

96 See *Lumen gentium*, no. 53.

CHAPTER 3

97   From the hymn *Ave Maris Stella*, ninth century. "Hail, bright star of ocean, / God's own Mother blest, / Ever sinless Virgin, / Gate of heavenly rest."

98   See the treatise by Salvatore M. Perrella, *Maria Vergine e Madre: La verginità feconda di Maria tra fede, storia e teologia* (Milano: San Paolo, Cinisello Balsamo, 2003).

99   Albert Mitterer, *Dogma und Biologie der heiligen Familie: nach dem Weltbild des Hl. Thomas von Aquin und dem der Gegenwart* (Wien: Herder, 1952).

100   Karl Rahner, *Virginitas in partu*, in Rahner, *Schriften zur Theologie*, IV (Einsiedeln: Benzinger, 1960), 173–205. For a reliable critique of this position, see the recent study by Fr. A. M. Apollonio, *Rilievi critici sulla mariologia di Karl Rahner* [*Critical remarks on Karl Rahner's Mariology*] in Fides Catholica II (2/2007): 438–57.

101   St. Ignatius, *Ad Smyrnensis*, 1, 1, FUNK 1, 273.

102   Cf. *DH* 503.

103   Raymond E. Brown, *The Birth of the Messiah: A Commentary on the Infancy Narratives the Gospels of Matthew and Luke* (New York: Doubleday, 1993).

104   Brown's conclusions on this data are in *The Birth of the Messiah*, 961–81.

105   Brown, *The Birth of the Messiah*, 540.

106   St. Jerome, *De perpetua virginitate S. Mariae adversus Elvidium*, 8 in *PL* 23, col. 201. St. Jerome deduces Mary's virginity at the birth of Jesus by the fact that *she herself* and not a midwife wraps the newborn in swaddling clothes. Hence, it can be inferred that Mary was not fatigued by the pain and consequences of a normal birth like other women and thus had no need of any assistance. The fiery St. Jerome is echoed later by, for example, Nicholas of Lyra (+1349), Juan Maldonado (+1583), and Augustin Calmet (1736). Of those who reject this element as "proof" of Mary's virginity at the birth, we have, besides Brown, Alfred Plummer, Konrad Schmid, and Jospeh A. Fitzmyer. See A. Serra, *E c'era la madre di Gesù...Saggi di esegesi biblico-mariana (1978-1988)*, Cens-Marianum, Cernusco sul Naviglio (Mi) 1989, 253–55.

107   St. Maximus the Confessor, *The Life of the Virgin*, 69. Interestingly, this Byzantine Father links the absence of labor pains at the moment of the birth with the absence of death pains at the time of Mary's Dormition because the Lord altered the course of nature in both cases (cf. 136).

108   For a general overview of the theme of the *virginitas in partu* see S. M. Perrella, *"La 'virginitas in partu:' status quaestionis"* (presentation, Atti del Convegno Internazionale di Studi Mariologici, Capua, Italy, May 19-24, 1992); P. D. Fehlner, *Signum Magnum: virginitas in partu. Nativitas D. N. J. C.* (Castelpetroso: Casa Mariana Editrice, 1995), 27.

109   See Andrew Welburn, *Myth of the Nativity: The Virgin Birth Re-examined* (Edinburgh: Floris Books, 2006).

110   Welburn is fundamentally convinced that the boundaries between ancient Christian literature, the Jewish tradition, and the ancient pagan mysteries are not so precise. Supposedly, there would be Gnostic interplay that would have influenced the beginnings of Christianity. See Andrew Welburn *The Beginnings of Christianity. Essene mystery, Gnostic revelation and the Christian vision* (Edinburgh: Floris Books, 2004).

111   Ruth Kara-Ivanov Kaniel, "The Myth of the Messianic Mother in Jewish and Christian Tradition: Psychoanalytic and Gender Perspectives," *Journal of the American Academy of Religion* 83, no. 1 (2015): 72-119. Starting with an examination of the Mother of the Messiah in Judaism and then in Christianity, and on the principal premise that the book of Ruth serves not just as an inter-textual conclusion of the entire history of the Davidic dynasty in the Old Testament but seems also to give form to the structure of the virgin birth in Matthew and Luke; in light of all this, the authoress wants to show that Mary's virginity would represent the "return of the repressed" in the Bible, since Mary would incarnate the model of the sexual sins of the mothers in the Davidic dynasty in an attempt to transform them into a model of virginity. By utilizing the Freudian myth of the "Egyptian Moses" (the return of the repressed and the memory of the "masculine sin" in the slaying of the primordial father), in Kaniel's view, Mary would represent the maternal and "feminine sin" in the Davidic genealogy. Her virginity would be an attempt to remedy it by overcoming the trauma. Apart from the gnostic admixture of psychoanalysis and theology, it is particularly striking to see the confused way in which the texts of the Fathers of the Church, alongside with certain truths like the Resurrection of Christ and the Assumption of our Lady, can be interpreted.

112   For a reliable exegesis within a critical framework of the famous text of Isaiah, see Stefano Manelli, *Mariologia biblica*, 37-52; W. G. Most, "New Light on the Messianic-Marian Character of Isaiah 7:14" *Miles Immaculatae* 25 (1989): 54-67. For a

Mariological overview on Our Lady's perpetual virginity taking into account all relevant scriptural texts, see Manfred Hauke, *Introduction to Mariology*, (CUA Press: Washington, D.C., 2021), 172-207.

113 St. Augustine, *Sermo 184: In Natale Domini*, I.1 in *PL* 38, coll. 995–96.

114 Ignace de la Potterie, "Il parto verginale del Verbo incarnato: 'Non ex sanguinibus... sed ex Deo natus est,'" *Marianum* 45 (1983): 174.

115 It is important to read the fierce critique by Padre Emanuele Testa, who carefully analyzed the studies of Brown, McKenzie, and the authors of the volume *Mary in the New Testament*, ed. Raymond E. Brown, Karl P. Donfried, Joseph Fitzmyer, and John Reumann (Philadelphia: Fortress Press, 1978); Emmanuele Testa, *Maria Terra Vergine: I rapporti della Madre di Dio con la SS. Trinità (I-IX centuries)*, vol. 1, Studium Biblicum Franciscanum Collectio Maior, vol. 31 (Jerusalem: Franciscan Printing Press, 1985), 209–21.

116 Raymond E. Brown, *The Birth of the Messiah*, 973.

117 *Ibid.*, 975–81.

118 *Ibid.*, 398.

119 *Ibid.*, 205.

120 *Ibid.*, 206–8.

121 *Ibid.*, 413, n. 3636.

122 *Ibid.*, 413.

123 Bultmann tried to de-mythologise the Scriptures and, in particular, the New Testament. A Christian could not be expected to welcome all mythical world pictures present in the New Testament, but in order to get to the very essence of the message, he proposed to overcome mythological events, as defined by him, including miracles. For him, in fact, it is not that important whether Christ is risen or not (the bodily resurrection can be a myth!) but the *kerigma* of faith coming from that event.

124 Donald A. Hagner, *Word Biblical Commentary: Matthew 1-13*, vol. 33A (Grand Rapids, MI: Zondervan, 2015), 57–58.

125 Pope Benedict XVI, *Jesus of Nazareth* (Milano: Rizzoli, 2007), 18–19.

126 René Laurentin, *I Vangeli del Natale* (Monferrato: Piemme Casale, 1987), 24–25.

127 In Jewish genealogies, there is never a reference to a woman. See Gen. 4; 5; 11. Only the father generates. Matthew and Luke are an exception.

128 Laurentin, *I Vangeli del Natale*, 19.

129   However, the fact that the Messiah, as St. Paul says, "was made to him of the seed of David, according to the flesh" (Rom. 1:3) leads one to believe that the Virgin Mary also belonged to the tribe of Judah and thus to the House of David, as well as the tribe of Levi because of her family ties with Elizabeth, wife of the High Priest Zachariah. This is sustained by Chromatius of Aquileia already in the fourth century. Cf. *Sermo XXIII*, 56–70, treatise I, 150–211; treatise II, 133–62. Also, St. Augustine, *Sermo 198/A*, in *Réa* 26 (1980) 70–72; St. Augustine, *The Consensus of the Evangelists*, 2.2.4, in *PL* 34, col. 1072.

130   Laurentin, *I Vangeli di Natale*, 44.

131   Cf. Peter Damien Fehlner, *Signum magnum: virginitas in partu. Nativitas D. N. J. C.*

132   Ignace de la Potterie, *Maria nel mistero dell'alleanza* (Genova: Marietti, 1992), 61.

133   St. Cyril of Jerusalem, *Catechesis 12*, 32 in *PG* 33, col. 765A.

134   Potterie, *Maria nel mister dell'alleanza*, 61–62. See also Aristide Serra, *E c'era la Madre di Gesù: saggi di esegesi biblico-mariana (1978-1988)* (Milan: Servitium Editrice, 1989), 255–57, wherein the author echoes de la Potterie's arguments, leaving the question open for future investigations to provide proof of validity, adding an important element in favor of Mary's virginity during the Birth: "The fact that Mary herself, and not anyone else, wraps the newborn Jesus in swaddling clothes, might imply that she gave birth in a 'holy' way, that is, free of any physical trauma which a woman is subject to during birth." Serra, *E c'era la madre di Gesù*, 257. It must also be said that the Fathers, especially the Eastern ones, saw the sign of the swaddling clothes as an important argument to underline the truth of the human nature assumed by Christ, against the error spread by Docetism. Serra, *E c'era la madre di Gesù*, 257–59. The theological rationale here cannot simply be ignored: if Christ is truly a man, Mary is truly a virgin.

135   For an exegesis and organic synthesis of the verses 12–14 of John's Prologue, see Manelli, *Mariologia biblica*, 153–61. See also John Dominic Crossan, "The Marian significance of John 1:12-13," in *De Beata Virgine Maria in Evangelio S. Ioannis et in Apocalypsi*, vol. 5, *Maria in Sacra Scriptura*, Acta Congressus Mariologici-Mariani in Republica Dominicana, anno 1965 celebrati (Rome: Pontificia Academia Mariana Internationalis, Romae, 1967), 99; Jean Galot, *Être ne' de Dieu: Jean 1:13* (Rome: Pontifical Biblical Institute, 1969); Jean Galot, "Maternità verginale di Maria e Paternità divina,"*La*

Civiltà Cattolica 139, no. 3 (1988): 209–22; Bernadette Escaffre
Ladet, "L'Evangile de Jean fait-il référence a la conception virginale?," *Ephermerides Mariologicae* 43 (1993): 349–65.

136   Ignace de la Potterie, "Il parto verginale del Verbo incarnato 'Non ex sanguinibus..., sed ex Deo natus est' (Gv 1, 13)," *Atti
della Settimana Sangue e Antropologia nella Letteratura Cristiana*,
vol. 2 (1983): 595–642. Pope John Paul II adopted this exegetical
hypothesis in the Catechesis of Wednesday, July 10, 1996. Cf. Perrella, *Maria Vergine e Madre*, 105. The interpretation in the singular of Jn 1:13, so as to prove the virginity of Mary "in partu", has
been recently confirmed by an excellent and detailed work: Denis
S. Kulandaisamy, *The Birth of Jesus or the Birth of Christians? An
Inquiry into the Authenticity of John 1:13*, (Marianum: Rome, 2015).

137   Serra, *E c'era la madre di Gesù*, 563. Cf. Aristride Serra,
"Vergine," in *Nuovo Dizionario di Mariologia*, ed. Stefano de Fiores
and Salvatore Meo (San Paolo: Cinisello Balsamo, 1996), 1281–1308.

138   Potterie, "*Il parto verginale del Verbo incarnato*," 163.

139   Cf. Potterie, 163.

140   Cf. Frédéric Manns, *Trenta domande (e trenta risposte) su
Maria e la nascita di Gesù* (Milan: Vita e Pensiero, 2007), 31–32.

141   That Mary had promised her virginity to God is a fact
dear to the Fathers of the Church, especially to St. Gregory of
Nyssa and St. Augustine: see Serra, "Vergine," *Nuovo Dizionario di Mariologia*. St. Maximus the Confessor also endorses the
interpretation of Mary's promise "to remain in virginity until her
death"; this is what has been "reported in the writings of the
pious Fathers." St. Maximus the Confessor, *The Life of the Virgin*,
53–54. For Ignace de la Potterie, Mary with her "I know not man"
manifests a strong desire for virginity, which is in contrast with
the ordinary Jewish mentality, even if it is not formulated as a vow.
See Potterie, *Maria nel mistero dell'alleanza*, 56–58. By contrast,
very surprisingly, Joseph Ratzinger writes thus in relation to the
question that Mary poses to the angel ("How is it possible? I know
not man"): "This question appears incomprehensible, since Mary
was betrothed and, according to Jewish law, was considered as
such to be a wife, even if she did not yet live with her husband
and the marital communion had still to begin. Since Augustine,
the explanation of the question has been that Mary had taken a
vow of virginity and had actuated the betrothal simply to have a
protector for her virginity. But this reconstruction is totally foreign
to the world of Judaism at the time of Jesus and seems unthinkable

in this context." *L'infanzia di Gesù* (Milano-Città del Vaticano: Rizzoli-LEV, 2012), 44–45. We said surprising because Ratzinger, in his triptych on Jesus, in effect seeks to go beyond an exegetic reading based unilaterally on the historical-critical method. Here, on the other hand, he seems to be relying strongly on it. In fact, if the vow or, rather, the promise Mary had made or the desire she had for virginity is unthinkable simply because it is foreign to Judaism at that time, how then can the virginal conception of Jesus in Mary's womb be explained? The virginity of Mary is the dawn of the Redemption. It is a new beginning.

142   St. Ambrose, *De institutione virginis*, 8.54 in *PL* 16, col. 320. Mary's womb, that gate which remained closed after the birth of Jesus, is also the Mariological reading that St. Maximus the Confessor makes of the Ezekiel prophecy: St. Maximus the Confessor, *The Life of the Virgin*, 76, 157.

143   For further references, see Manelli, *Mariologia biblica*, 89–94; Brunero Gherardini, *La Madre* (Frigento: Casa Mariana Editrice, 2007), 110–11.

144   *DH* 422. Subsequently to the Lateran Council of 649, convened by Pope Martin I, the perpetual virginity of Mary is defined dogmatically with the following formula: "If anyone does not, following the holy Fathers, confess properly and truly that holy Mary, ever virgin and immaculate, is Mother of God, since in this latter age she conceived really and truly, without human seed, from the Holy Spirit, God the Word himself, who before the ages was born of God the Father, and gave birth to Him without corruption, her virginity remaining equally inviolate after the birth, let him be condemned."

145   St. Epiphanius, *Panarion 78*, 6 in *PG* 42, col. 705.

146   St. Augustine, *Sermo 186*, 1.1 in *PL* 38, col. 999.

147   On the question of the "brothers" and sisters" of Jesus, see also Manelli, *Mariologia biblica*, 387–90, which is based principally on the study by Josef Blinzler, *I fratelli e le sorelle di Gesù* (Brescia: Paideia, 1975).

148   St. Irenaeus, *Adversus haereses*, IV.33.11 in *PG* 7, col. 830.

CHAPTER 4

149   St. Leo the Great, *Sermo 7, De Nativitate Domini*. "Wherefore, when we draw near to understand the mystery of Christ's Birth, wherein He was born of the Virgin Mary, we must leave the clouds of earthly imagination behind."

150 On the theological virginity of Mary, see Luis Ángel Montes Peral, "Hablar de Maria hoy," *Ephemerides Mariologicae* 58 (2008): 115–16. As I consider Mary's theological virginity as archetype, I readily refer precisely to the mystery of Mary's virginity, and on other occasions more generally to the mystery of "Mary," as almost interchangeable, given the fulfillment of the mystery of perpetual virginity in her person. I intend to speak of "Mary the Virgin," interchanging the name with the nominal adjective.

151 Manns, *Trenta domande (e trenta risposte) su Maria e la nascita di Gesù*, 29.

152 St. Augustine seems to allude to the parallel between the bodily nature of Mary's virginity and the bodily nature of Christ's Resurrection when he writes, "It cannot therefore appear magical that the flesh of a man was born of a virgin, since only the flesh of Christ came forth in this way, as is also not magical the fact that only the flesh of Christ resurrected on the third day and will never die any more. Otherwise, all of God's miracles would be the works of magic since they only happened once." *Contra Faustum manichaeum*, 29.2 in *PL* 8, col. 489. In Raymond Brown, the bodily resurrection of Christ is defended as the announcement of the new creation and of the resurrection of the flesh, while the question of Mary's bodily virginity is left open. *La concezione verginale e la risurrezione corporea di Gesù* (Brescia: Queriniana, 1977). It seems to us a rather conflicting vision: failing to recognize clearly the bodily nature of Mary's virginity would lead eventually to the denial of the bodily nature of Christ's Resurrection and the consequent new creation in which the spiritual bodies will live. What sign would Christ give of His Resurrection in His very own body if one excludes the physical and historical truth of the Ever-Virgin Mary? All the miracles of Christ would indeed be magical. Gregory the Great is a witness to this in his homily on the Gospel of John (20:19–31). When asking himself how the real, resurrected body of Christ could possibly enter the Cenacle with all the doors shut, he makes the connection between the truth of the bodily Resurrection with that of the virginal birth. He says, "The body of Christ entered where His disciples were behind closed doors, so that, to the human eye, by way of His nativity, He came forth from the closed womb of the Virgin. It would in fact be strange that after His Resurrection, already victorious in eternity, He that entered through closed doors would not have come forth from the closed womb of the Virgin." *Homiliarium in Evangelia*, 1.II, Homilia XXVI in *PL* 76, coll. 1197–98.

153 Manns, *Trenta domande (e trenta risposte) su Maria e la nascita di Gesù*, 33.

154 Cf. Vatican Council II, dogmatic constitution on the Church *Lumen Gentium* (November 21, 1964), no. 63.

155 K. L. Schmidt, "Basileuo," in *Grande Lessico del Nuovo Testamento*, ed. Gerhard Kittel, vol. 2 (Brescia: Paideia, 1966), col. 186.

156 Schmidt, "Basileuo," col. 188.

157 *Commentaria* in Mt 14:7.

158 Schmidt, "Basileuo," coll. 200–3. See also the enlightened reflection on the Kingdom of God with all its implications by Pope Benedict XVI, *Gesù di Nazaret*, 69–86.

159 See *Catechism of the Catholic Church* (Rome: Libreria Editrice Vaticana, 1992), nos. 551–53. Congregation for the Doctrine of the Faith, Declaration on the Unicity and Salvific Universality of Jesus Christ and the Church *Dominus Iesus* (August 6, 2000), nn. 18–19.

160 Rudolf Schnackenburg, *Signoria e Regno di Dio* (Bologna: Il Mulino, 1971), 79–80.

161 Schnackenburg, 122.

162 St. Augstine, *De sancta virginitate*, 2.2 in *PL* 6, col. 397.

163 Dionigi Tettamanzi, *La verginità per il Regno: Dalle catechesi di Giovanni Paolo II* (Milan: Edizioni OR, 1982), 17.

164 "So great was Mary's grace, that she not only kept the gift of virginity for herself, but she gave the ornament of integrity also to those that she visited." St. Ambrose, *De institutione virginis*, 7.50 in *PL* 16, col. 319.

165 See Giulia P. di Nicola and Attilio Danese, *Verginità e matrimonio: Reciprocità e diversità* (Cinisello Balsamo: Edizioni San Paolo, 2000); *La reciprocità verginità-matrimonio. Profezia di comunione nella Chiesa Sposa* (Siena: Edizioni Cantagalli, 2000).

EPILOGUE

166 St. Ambrose, *Comment on Luke's Gospel*, 2,19 in *PL* 15, col. 1573. "Among all that are born of women the Lord Jesus Christ stood alone in holiness. Fresh from His immaculate Birth, He felt no contagion from human corruption, . . . Who also alone hath opened the secret womb of His holy Virgin the Church, filling her with a sinless fruitfulness to give birth to Christian souls."

167 St. Augustine, *Contra Faustum manichaeum*, 29.4 in *PL* 8, col. 491.

168 St. Augustine, *De sancta virginitate*, 2.2 in *PL* 6, col. 397.

169   St. Francis of Assisi, "Saluto alla Beata Vergine" in *Fonti Francescane*, ed. Biblioteca francescana di Milano (Assisi: Edizioni Messaggero, 1980), nn. 259–60.

170   "O name that does my heart inebriate, / Embosomed in pure heavenly delight, / Whose beauty spurs my soul to jubilate, / Both night and day may I your love requite."

ABOUT THE AUTHOR

FR SERAFINO M. LANZETTA STD is resident in the Diocese of Portsmouth (England) where he exercises his priestly ministry. He is lecturer in Dogmatic Theology at the Theological Faculty of Lugano (Switzerland) and editor-in chief of the Theological Journal *Fides Catholica*. He has facilitated the organisation of several Theological Conferences — the last one on The Fatima Message in its 100th Anniversary, and has written for *L'Osservatore Romano*. His published works include his post-doctoral habilitation, *Vatican II, a Pastoral Council: Hermeneutics of Council Teaching* (Gracewing, 2016), *Fatima at the Heart of the Church: God's Vision of History and Oblative Spirituality* (2018), *The Symphony of Truth: Theological Essays* (Arouca Press, 2020) and *The Door of Faith* (Arouca Press, 2022).